I0161577

CONTINUITIES

The South in a Time of Revolution

JOHN DEVANNY

Continuities: The South in a Time of Revolution

Copyright© 2022 John Devanny

Produced in the Republic of South Carolina by

SHOTWELL PUBLISHING LLC
Post Office Box 2592
Columbia, So. Carolina 29202
www.ShotwellPublishing.com

Cover Image: *Live Oaks in South Carolina* by Thomas Addison Richards c.1858. Wikimedia Commons Public Domain

ISBN: 978-1-947660-86-1

FIRST EDITION

10 9 8 7 6 5 4 3 2 1

TABLE OF CONTENTS

FOREWORD

The occasional essay was long a well-regarded feature of Anglo-American literature. Though anticipated perhaps in the multitude of pamphlets in the 17th century, it took definite form in Addison's and Steele's *The Tatler* and *The Spectator* of the early 18th century. This was followed by the great quarterly reviews of the 19th century. These were written and read by people of wide learning and interests, but, alas, have been largely replaced by superficial "news" and jargon-filled "scholarly" journals.

The occasional essay was characterised by its personal and conversational style. It dealt usually with things of contemporary interest but with an insight and humane attention superior to ordinary discussion. It wore its considerable learning lightly and sometimes revealed a little gentle humour.

John Devanny's work in a form so rare these days exemplifies that great tradition in letters. One comes away from the reading with the satisfaction of having engaged in a civilised conversation and gained new insight into our world.

Clyde N. Wilson

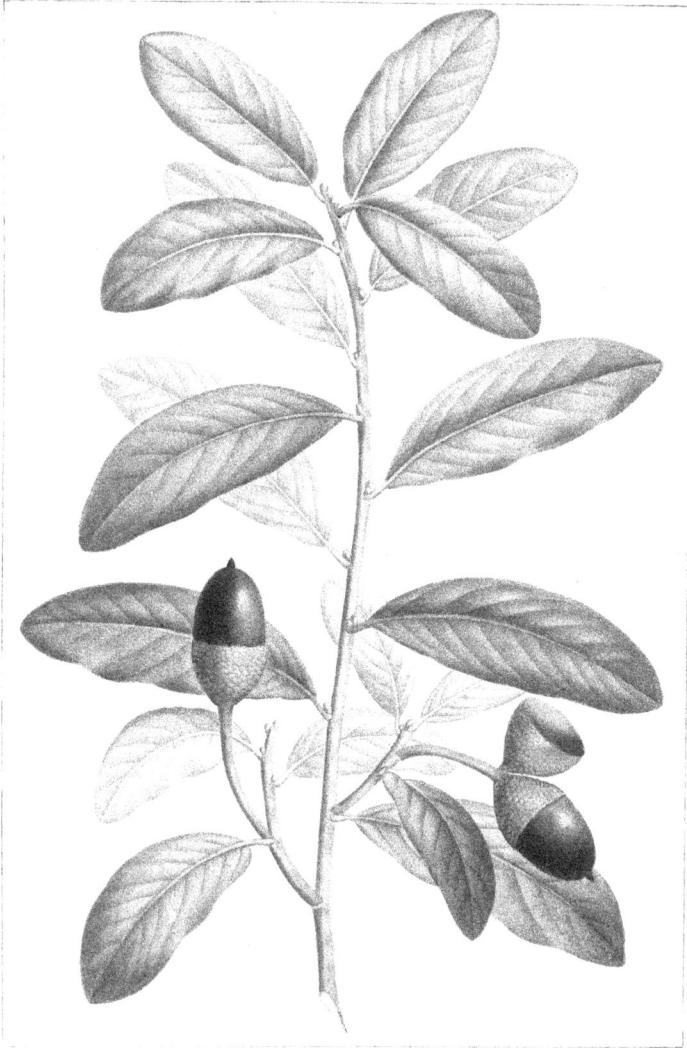

PREFACE

Conservative is a term fraught with an elasticity of meaning in our time. The various and sundry groups and individuals who populate the "conservative movement" do not, as the late political theorist Willmoore Kendall put it, keep house together. My purpose in bringing these various essays together is not to add one more voice to the babel, but to comment upon those things held dear by conservatives who live south of Mason's and Dixon's line. The book's themes: faith, place, family, custom, tradition, and of course continuity are all a part of the traditional concerns of Southern conservatives. These concerns are intimately connected to some important truths about the lives of men and women. We all live under constraints which are very real, the constraints imposed by original sin, namely concupiscence and darkened intellects. Such a statement in our time may be viewed by many as horribly reactionary, or even superstitious. Yet the events of history and contemporary times prove their truth. The Southern conservative certainly felt the weight of these burdens on the human condition, for this reason he has ever been suspicious of abstraction and utopian schemes and their promoters. He casts a cold eye upon all such and has in mind the question of the ancient Romans, *cui bono?* To the self-appointed guardians of equity and justice, he rightly asks who shall be their guardians? Ever is he inclined to leave matters at rest, ever is he on guard against the marriage of sentiment and utopia, knowing all too well the progeny of that union is the concentration camp, the gulag, and the gas chamber.

In our day, the Christian faith, tradition, custom, family, and place are under murderous assault from a wealthy and powerful elite who are joined to nothing but their schemes. These essays, hopefully, may offer some moment's rest. Change is certainly part of the human condition, but only a part. Continuities surround us, in the exploration of our culture, history, and politics we have the feeling that we have been here before, because in a way we have. The costumes, fashions, and surface issues may change, human nature and the great contest between those who would limit and those who would expand the powers of the state remain.

In one other way the Southern conservative tradition is unique. In addition to the aforementioned concerns, the Southern conservative is a philosophical realist, which is to say that he does not believe that reality resides in an emotion, an abstract form or ideal in some never never land, or is subjected to the ideological fashion of the day. No, he believes that reality resides in the thing itself. The South is still, though just barely, Christian because the Incarnation makes sense to her people. Whatever Christianity's faults may be in the South, and they are legion, it is doubtful she would have ever fallen prey to the great Christological heresies of the first three centuries of the Church's existence. It is little wonder that Saint Thomas Aquinas's, *Summa Theologica* occupied a place in many of the libraries of the South's protestant clergy. It is this reflexive commitment to the reality of things that keeps the South more resistant than some other regions to the violations and abuses of the natural law, to prudence, and to right reason.

This modest collection is designed to express the *mentalité* of a Southern conservative who holds to the old verities of faith and family, place, tradition, and custom. And who views history, and politics, and culture through the lens of not just changes, but important continuities.

Musings on Dislocation

Dislocation brings with it a dissonance. Moving disrupts the consonance of time and place, of family, friends, parish, and all the landmarks and milestones that speak to us of our country, that is our homes. On the Feast of the Holy Family (old calendar), December 29, 2013, this reality of dislocation and dissonance intruded upon my family and me. We removed from our home in the upcountry of South Carolina to Winston-Salem, leaving behind our gardens, our blueberry orchard, trees we had planted, our parish, innumerable good friends, and the past events of our family's sojourn in the lands west of the Saluda River.

In dislocating, we were no different from millions of Americans and Southerners throughout history. Thomas Jefferson and James Madison, among others, believed centuries might be needed to fill up the continent; Americans perpetually on the move westward proved them wrong. The social costs of mobility have been high. Soil exhaustion from careless tillage, boom towns gone bust, the weakening of ties among kith and kin, the emergence of rust belt cities, all attest to these costs. The political costs are no less worrisome, for if the common good does exist, and those who are small "r" republicans can hardly attest otherwise, it must by the nature of human existence exist in a place. Speaking of the globalists in his day, John Randolph of Roanoke said of his manufacturing opponents in the debate over the 1816 tariff that he "feared those men." Why? Because they were the "citizens of no place." The migration of American manufacturing and capital overseas thirty years ago underscores Mr. Randolph's observation.

We who must dislocate because of necessity must never choose the path of irresponsibility, the dehumanizing fate of becoming citizens of no place, nor should our attachment to place be mere nostalgic sentiment. Like the practical-minded Southern thinkers throughout the ages, John Taylor of Caroline, Edmund Ruffin, and a younger and wiser Wendell Berry come to mind, we too must work and hope for that attachment to place, from which shall spring the revival of faith, agriculture, and vibrant local communities from which an enduring revival of a virtuous political culture might spring.

I and my family, who are among the wandering bands of education professionals, what do folks like us do? The vegetable garden is planted, strawberries and blueberries are ordered for fall planting, and we get out to meet the new neighbors. We work on long neglected essays, the house, the education of our children, and assist at the Mass in the old classical Latin rite down in Salisbury. We take consolation in the reality that we are all wanderers and pilgrims here on this earth, at least in the mortal sense, for the earth is the permanent home of no one individual man or woman. We attend to the tasks of our state in life with diligence and care, and when we fail, we own up to our failure, when we sin, we seek forgiveness. And, if we must leave again, we hope, pray, and act to leave the old homestead a place better than we found it, for those who shall stay.

Fall Planting

The fall vegetable garden is a delight in the Mid-South. The greens and reds are vivid. Fresh lettuce and beans will grace the table until the first heavy frosts; even beyond if we are fortunate and blessed. Spinaches, cabbages, broccoli, collards, mustard greens, and radishes will yield through the Christmas season. Garlic, onions, and shallots will repose through the winter, then burst forth in spring with their abundance. No vegetable is sweeter than that which is fall harvested. The harsh summer heat releases its hold, the nights cool, and soft autumn rains allow the plow and hoe to shape the new beds for strawberries, weather and time yield to the fall planting. As nature slowly slides to its annual death, fall planting remains a quiet, yet defiant act in the face of winter. Even more than the spring garden, the gardens of fall smell of hope and reaffirm Virgil's old saying, *Dum vita est spes est.*

Fall is fickle in the border South; she is rarely on time—too early or too late, all glorious splendor then done. Delaware, Maryland, Kentucky, and the hill country of Missouri–too soon they will feel the heavy gray clouds, or the pale, squinty suns of winter. Autumn is brief in the borderlands. In the Carolinas, fall planting is akin to the summer party conversation winding down, the company becoming reflective, we so do wish the celebration to remain; we strain at arresting its departure. By contrast, in the border states fall planting is hurried in summer's heat, the harvests are full, but brief; the freezes often early and sharp, so every trick of the trade is used to keep alive that which keeps us alive.

Fall, I believe, loves best the Carolina Piedmont. I have never known her to be early or late there. She arrives with the equinox, and then lingers on through much of Advent, often even to the Golden Christmases Mr. William Gilmore Simms of South Carolina so heartily praised. There is no rude or boisterous entrance into the lives of Carolinians as Marylanders or Virginians in the lower Shenandoah must endure. Fall has learned her manners and the civilized arts by the time she reaches the South Carolina Upcountry.

Under Fall's hand, nature slowly and gently recedes to her winter sleep: the putting forth of roots by trees, the drowsy glance touching the south bound waterfowl, and the faint stirring of crisp mornings roused fully awake by the bark and clamor of rabbit or bird dogs in the field. Fall never wishes to leave the Carolina Piedmont; only reluctantly does she give way to the dreary winter, and in the Upcountry of South Carolina, she often holds winter at bay until the very arrival spring.

In the fall we plant with the expectation of rich and full harvests. Yes, we hope for the succulence of spinach, the sweet collards sautéed in garlic butter and served with bacon and cayenne sauce. Mounds of broccoli dressed in Hollandaise or lemon butter seduce our palates, as does the sweet beans cooked slow with fatback. But other things are planted in the fall as well. We plant ideas, stories, and the cardinal virtues, in the minds, hearts, and imaginations of our families, neighbors, and students, what wiser generations once called tradition. Hopefully, we also plant the spiritual and corporal works of mercy, so that the theological virtues may bloom and grace from heaven may be harvested and savored. Hospitality we also hope to both plant and harvest, especially as the holydays draw nigh. All this done in the long and lingering goodbye of our dear cousin fall before she too must give way to the rude imposition of time.

M.R. Ducks

Years ago, I was first introduced to my wife's grandmother to elicit the approval of the family matriarch of our impending marriage. This small but formidable woman lived in Columbus, Ohio, a descendant of tough, blue collar, shanty Irish. We got to talkin' about the tragic experience of the Irish in the northern environs of America, the Democratic Party's abandonment of regular folk, why you never can really trust a Republican, and would not it be great if Pat Buchanan became president. She was tough and two-fisted and would have fit in well with some of the tough and two-fisted characters I knew from Baltimore.

Later in the evening my wife told me that her grandmother approved; her sole reservation about me was, "that boy talks Southern." Indeed "Grumpma," as she was affectionately known by my wife's family, had explained to me earlier that her people in central Ohio did not trust Southerners. Their charm, polish, and manners hid deep and dark designs. I took no offense since I was distrustful of fast-talking and rude Yankees. But Grumpma's comment on my talking Southern was curious.

Truth be told, my accent is a cross between "Bawlmorese," the softer sounds of the Southern Maryland tidewater, and some sprinklings of South Carolina's piedmont region from my long residence in the Palmetto state. Nothing unusual here, Maryland until recent times was a melting pot of dialects and accents where one could hear the flat sounds of Pennsylvania's midlands accent, the soft tidewater lilt and slur, the hard r's and flat a's of Appalachia, some old Cornwall sounds from the islands in the Chesapeake, all spiced with either low country Carolina or Brooklyn bravado from immigrants south and north. A few years back I attended a reception hosted by the Maryland General Assembly's Hunting Coalition. Mostly these were older gents, so sure enough, every Maryland accent and dialect was present in the room, even in this age homogenized of Valley Girl speak. It was a wonderful linguistic smorgasbord, a marvel that such a small state might have so many ways of talkin.'

In the old days, Maryland accents south of the Patapsco sounded a bit like Robert Mitchum's character, Max Cady in the film *Cape Fear*—Southern velvet with a hard edge. Not so long ago one could tell what part of the city of Baltimore a person came from by listening to how he pronounced the city's name. In general, "Bawlmer" pegged you as someone from the east side, "Balteemore" from the westside, if you lived in Roland Park and attended a toney school like Bryn Mawr, you said Băltǐmòre (very proper), from the south side of town people said Baldamor, and those of us who lived south of the Patapsco, the non-rhotic, soft consonant Balmoh. As populations have changed and folks get more mobile these differences no longer exist in the stark fashion of yesteryear, but they are still there if you go looking for them.

Points further south of Maryland exhibit a linguistic diversity just as rich. The genteel class of the tidewater and low country South speak what is for my money the most beautiful form of English in the world. Not all Southerners talk slow; I have heard Southerners in the piedmont speak in a staccato clip that might leave a New Yorker breathless. Add to this the deep rich tones of the delta in Mississippi, the flat intonations of Cajun speak, the mysteries of Gullah speech, and the thousand and one other variations of speech and dialect that I am slighting, and one must conclude that talkin' Southern is the most complex of linguistic gumbos. Thus, folks in the North might think I talk Southern, but to the ears of many an upcountry South Carolinian, my voice carries the tones of a Yankee. Mind, one could be a native Charlestonian and the upcountry Carolinians would still insist that yes, that person too sounds like a Yankee. This point was made to me by a fellow graduate student at USC (The real USC, not that whippersnapper on the Left Coast.) who related the story of a female teacher from Charleston who made her way to the wilds of Due West, South Carolina to teach the heathen Presbyterian. She was immediately pegged as a Yankee, which is to say a barbarian, for like the ancient Greeks the sturdy sons of the Piedmont only heard "bar, bar, bar" when she spoke.

It will surely be a shame if the current rage for cultural homogenization carries these beautiful ways of speaking away from us. Dialect, you see, is more than inflection, lilt, and tongue placement. It is indicative of how we view the world and our place in it, dialect and accent transmits our culture and pace of life through time and space via sound. A "diversity" that celebrates many colors, one sound, and one way of thinking is awful bland at best, like having vanilla, chocolate, and peppermint all taste the same. Sameness has about it the tyranny and desolation of a desert.

No, I wish to hear the long multiple vowels and soft consonants of Southern coastal speech, people who live in heat and humidity should talk that way. When I am in the hill country, I want to hear Scotch-Irish twangs, out west give me a Texas drawl that moves with the slow thunder of a cattle drive. Me, I want all the flavors of the Southland. For instance, how dull if in an Eastern Shore duck blind, we hear a conversation that goes like this,

> *"Those are ducks.*
> *No they are not.*
> *Oh, yes they are.*
> *See their wings?*
> *Well I'll be.*
> *Those are ducks!"*
> So much better to hear,
> *"M. R. Ducks*
> *M.R. Not*
> *O. S. A. R.*
> *C. M. Wangs*
> *L. I. B.*
> *M. R. Ducks."*

Football and the South

Are you ready?

Hell yea!

Damn right!

Hotty Toddy, gosh almighty,

Who the hell are we?

HEY!

Flim Flam, Bim Bam, OLE MISS BY DAMN!

WARNNING: Blasphemy ahead.

College football has long cast a powerful spell upon the minds and hearts of the people below Mason's and Dixon's line. Team flags fly from cars and porches declare the citizenship of the resident as a member of the Gamecock nation, Gator nation, assorted Tiger nations, and all other nations that populate the lands of the SEC, ACC, the Southern Conference, and all the rest. Some of these homes are houses of divided loyalties, quite common in Florida, South Carolina, and Alabama. New residents of towns in the South are greeted with the question, "Are you a Gamecock, a Bulldog, or a Tiger?" A bit of a new take on "Who are your people?" The stadia where our gladiators ply their trade are sacred shrines presided over by men who possess the most treasured title in the South, the title "Coach." These temples and shrines are the scenes of past triumphs, agonizing cathartic defeat, and eternal springs of hope. Ah yes, college football in the South, ain't nuthin' like it.

Now, dear reader, before you dismiss me as one more book-worm casting sarcastic, envy-laden aspersions and blasphemies upon football, that most Southern of religions, a bit of disclosure might be in order. In high school I played football and lacrosse.

Later in college, and a little beyond, I played rugby (American football's Daddy)—and I have enjoyed a few bouts of what we might call "recreational boxing." So I know from experience all about two a days in the August heat and humidity, Friday night lights, and the ringing of bells—mine and others.

What I have come to realize is, traditionally speaking, football just ain't all that Southern. Consider the following: American football is an odd blend of various "football games" resembling variations of soccer and rugby. These games were played in such disparate locales as prep schools in the north, the Ivy League schools, and among the toughs who worked the steel mills, iron foundries, and coal mines of western Pennsylvania and eastern Ohio. The father of American football was not Bear Bryant (Gasp!), but a Connecticut Yankee from Yale by the name of Walter Camp. It gets worse. Professor Andrew Doyle of Winthrop University, the true master of this sort of sports arcana, observes that football was the game of the industrial machine age. Indeed, at the turn of the last century, many Southern parsons and Daddies were adamantly opposed to having their young ones play a "damned Yankee" factory game. Some of these parsons suggested baseball as a more "bucolic" alternative. All too bad since baseball was a Yankee and city-boy game as well. Alexander Cartwright, the father of modern baseball, was the New Yorker who first codified the rules of the game. Even worse, well worse for some folks anyway, the game of baseball can trace its earliest origins to late medieval France.

Oh, I do grant you dear reader that the South tried ridiculously hard to both baptize and deep-fry football. Professor Doyle assures us that Southerners adopted football as their own to win redemption for grandaddy's whuppin' at Gettysburg. Every fan knew the Almighty rooted for their side, every great coach was another Bobby Lee, every great back a Jeb Stuart, and every game against a team from up North was another Vicksburg—but with the appropriate ending this time around. The South, in a charming Walter Scott sort of way, promoted marching bands, homecoming courts, and of course cheerleaders. Fans attended games in semi-formal attire back in the day—like going to church. All these trappings made the college game, as played in the South, resemble an odd blend of a well-heeled Episcopal service and a jousting tournament in the waning days of the middle-ages, just as gunpowder was coming into its own. It was all a far cry from the way the boys whose last names began with "Mc" or ended in "ski" played the game in its early years. And as the South enjoyed more success on the "old gridiron" (Gridiron, it doesn't even sound Southern, does it?), it showed the rest of the nation that it had arrived in the modern, progressive, swinging world of state-sponsored, industrial capitalism.

So dear reader, you may be thinking, "If football really ain't so Southern, at least in the traditional sense, then what sports are?" The blood sports dear reader, the blood sports. With respect to the sporting life, Thomas Jefferson once advised a nephew that,

"A strong body makes the mind strong. As to the species of exercise, I advise the gun. While this gives a moderate exercise to the body, it gives boldness, enterprise, and independence to the mind. Games played with the ball, and others of that nature, are too violent for the body, and stamp no character on the mind. Let your gun therefore be the constant companion of your walks."

One might also add fishing and horse racing, the last being a particular favorite of Mr. Jefferson.

What is truly important in all this flippancy is that sports are an interesting barometer of society. Jefferson's choice of recreation is the choice of an Old Republican. Agrarian republics need men (and women) who are bold, enterprising, and independent. Why? Because these are precisely the traits people possess who are capable of self-government, and who possess character, rather than being a character. What then is the football fanatic capable of? Good question—these days it involves alcohol, obesity, nudity, and body paint.

Does this mean then that if the South abandons her love affair with college football that all will be right in Dixie? No, that would be like throwing out the thermometer to get rid of the fever. But dear reader we might ask ourselves the question why some of us may care more about our football teams than we do our families, our neighbors, and our country? Then we might just begin to diagnose some of the maladies that truly afflict us.

How 'bout a Little
Bourbon with Your Philosophy?

What exactly makes the South, the South? Hosts of scholars have puzzled mightily over this one. Historians might point to the old Confederacy, human geographers might look for the proliferation of Southern Baptist Churches, as well as clusters and distributions of BBQ joints and firearms ownership, while linguists ponder over the prevalence of "y'all" and other Southern speech patterns. The Academy is a bit nervous, for you see, the South is slowly disappearing. This means producing new villains, and even more hysterical fulminations on how slavery in the southern United States is the root of all evil: past, present, and future. Yes, there is grant money and tenure at stake here too, though one might justly believe that the South has been studied and analyzed into an early grave. But really the South, however ill-defined, does seem to be disappearing.

Let us have the evidence you say. Well, here goes. The snow geese migration has taken a heavy toll on traditional voting patterns in Maryland beginning in the 1970s, current day Virginia and North Carolina, not to say anything of Atlanta and Florida, but that of course goes back to carpetbagging days. Southern Democrats in the mold of Virginia Senator Carter Glass, Governor Ritchie of Maryland, and other Jeffersonian types are extinct. Southern accents are disappearing. Case in point, the midlands accent of New Jersey and Pennsylvania once extended to the area north of Baltimore, now it is firmly entrenched throughout most of Maryland and northern Virginia. Just find a linguistic map from 1970 and compare it to one from 2010. In my teaching career, the sons and daughters of people born and bred in South Carolina sport the accents of the San Fernando Valley. "Like, really?" "Yes, Tiffany, really." There was a time, as far north as Baltimore, that when you ordered iced tea, it came sweetened; now we all must specifically ask for "sweet tea" in all places south of Mason and Dixon's line. The list could go on *ad infinitum*. And truth be told, much of what we take as "Southern" since the Late Unpleasantness is of dubious heritage. Tent revivals, fundamentalism, bible colleges, football, textiles, are Northern imports one and all.

So let us join Boethius, not the bird dog but the philosopher, who wrote *The Consolation of Philosophy*, and pour ourselves a bourbon (on a bit of crushed ice please) and find some consolation in our philosophizing about this predicament. Indeed, we are already fortunate for poor Boethius only had philosophy for consolation, and we have bourbon as well.

We might begin by considering why we might begin to miss such things as Southern accents (all thirteen or so of them, there ain't just one), sweet tea, tobacco fields, and such. These things, indeed, all the familiar voices, places, people, cuisine, and habits are the temporal, and at times sacred, signposts of our lives and the lives of our society. These things work their way into our very being. As beings both temporal and spiritual, we carry within ourselves the marriage of the temporal and spiritual. To wax theological a moment, the whole point of the hypostatic union was to marry the divine to the temporal so that the latter might be raised out of the whole mess of original and actual sin. What makes the South, "the South," is the substance embodied in voice, sight, smell, and taste. This substance is something more than an ephemeral form (God preserve us from the "America is an idea" and "The South is an idea" types). The substance is married to blood and soil, to the temporal beings who encounter its existence. Whatever the sights and smells of the part of the South from which you hail, these contain within themselves the substances of the virtues to which they are married. A Christmas Eve duck hunt in the Chesapeake tidewater does not merely evoke or call to mind friendship, civility, and hospitality, these are intimately bound together to the thing itself. The same can be said for the local pig pickin' in North Carolina, the parish shrimp boil in Louisiana, and the oyster roast in the South Carolina low country.

These marriages of the temporal and spiritual were not made *ex nihilio*. The ancestors of those who would live in the South encountered a land that they viewed as a garden, not a wilderness upon which to erect cities on the hills. Too often some Southerners and their descendants failed in their duties to the garden and its original inhabitants, but many tended the garden with skill and care, and befriended and married its natives. Many Southerners purchased the sons and daughters of Africa, and many committed grave cruelties upon them, but many also lived with, supported, and worked side by side with their bondsmen. Whatever his faults regarding slavery, the Southerner never found the existence of Africans in his world *per se* a scandal, that foolishness had its roots in regions further north. The Southerner had a high tolerance for the "imperfections" of the natural world and the society in which he lived; he acknowledged the existence of constraints.

If then we can locate a fundamental distinction in America between the archetypical Southerner and the archetypical Yankee, it is that the former attempted to conform his mind and existence to reality whereas the latter hoped to bend reality to the abstract products of his mind. This latter position is a horrifying philosophical mistake. It suggests the eulogy delivered at Robert Kennedy's funeral given by his brother Edward Kennedy when the younger Kennedy said of his dead brother that, "He dreamed of things that never were and asked why not?" Such a statement might be taken as a symptom of insanity for its denial of constraint, limit, and the existence of the Creator's design. The Southerner was, and a number of them still are, philosophical realists, or as Flannery O'Connor put it, "hillbilly Thomists." That is why the natural world was so important to the Southern way of life. The world was real, not a playground for the abstractions of secular Puritans or neo-Platonic fantastics. The hillbilly Thomist conforms his mind to reality, seeks to improve what can be improved, ameliorate what can be ameliorated, and endure what cannot be changed. He embraces reality, not virtual reality. We need more hillbilly Thomists. Otherwise, the task of preserving what is noble, good, and true in the Southern tradition will be an even more daunting task.

The slow disappearance of Southern manners, speech patterns, rural life, cuisine and all the rest are disturbing because these are so intimately tied to a peculiar (at least peculiar in the American context) Southern acknowledgement of reality. Thus, the fading of accents, mores, and *ethos* are not the mere fading of veneer, but the withering of substance. When Richard Weaver remarked that the American South was the last non-material civilization in the West, he based this on his observation that Southern piety was founded on the inscrutability of nature and providence. From this orientation flowed the old virtues of hospitality, friendship, respect for place and hierarchy, and release from envy. In such a place evil might be tolerated longer than some thought seemly, but for all that, it would be hard to discover a finer country.

> Hey darlin', fetch me another please and make it a double
> —the company are stayin' awhile.

Gentleman Bob and the Decline of the South

Coal miners have their canaries; we have *colinus virginiánus*, the bobwhite quail. Like the canary that goes silent as the oxygen levels in a mine drop, so too has the quail gone silent in large swaths of the South. Like the silence of the canary, the absence of Gentlemen Bob bodes ill for the health of the Southern countryside and the rural communities it contains.

The decline of Gentleman Bob has been attributed to a number of factors. Wildlife biologists blame the loss and destruction of favorable habitat. Some point to diseases and parasites as the true ravagers of the quail. Myself, I lay the blame at a number of doors. The small farms with their hedgerows and weedy edges, where people, crops, and quail thrived have gone missing, replaced by road to road "clean" cultivation. As these habitats began to disappear, wildlife agencies began a curious love affair with such varmints as hawks, coyotes, and wolves. The decline of trapping among the younger generation after the 1960s may have been celebrated heartily in many a fox den, PETA den, and raccoon nest, but not so much by Gentleman Bob who now had more worries to add to his list. Loss of habitat, the ever expanding suburban savannah and its one inch cut putting green lawns, and game laws that favored predators over prey have left Gentlemen Bob in a bad way.

Well, too bad for Gentlemen Bob you might say, and if you are truly enlightened you might also think too bad for the men and women who hunt quail and the dogs they follow in the field. But what exactly, you might ask, has this to with the state of things in Dixie? Well, much dear reader.

You see, Gentlemen Bob thrives where country people thrive. By thrive I do not mean $40,000 pick-up trucks that haul one person and some air in the back. Nor do I mean satellite TV, vacations to Maui, or a lifetime supply of Doritos and Viagra. I do mean the ownership and good stewardship of land in such a fashion as to provide a sufficiency for the people who derive their livelihood from it, and a surplus to aid posterity and the less fortunate. I also mean the fostering of independence over false security, charity over materialism, stewardship over exploitation. No doubt, Bayer, Archer Daniel Midlands, and Syngenta (a subsidiary owned by ChemChina no less) prefer the dependence of rural America upon their products and their genetically modified seeds that cannot be saved. But this is not the vision Jefferson had for the independent and self-sufficient farmer as the bulwark of the republic.

Since the end of the Late Unpleasantness, the farmer in the South, and his brethren elsewhere have struggled with the prevailing trends in finance, demographics, and politics that have subordinated his avocation to the mores and methods of finance, industry, and biotechnology. Farmland is bid up well beyond the means of young aspiring farmers—who can outbid Bill Gates, Ted Turner, and China? Most of the agricultural practices taught at land grant universities and encouraged by Agric. Inc. do lead to incredible harvests, but also to the need for government subsidy and come at the loss of more topsoil each year. Truth be told, some of the larger farmers have also to struggle with their concupiscence, as do we all, the cold cruelty of "get big or get out" fuels the avarice to acquire evermore land and capital.

The destruction of the family farm was given a major boost by the Republican party during the administration of Richard M. Nixon. Nixon's Secretary of Agriculture, Earl Butz (in some quarters pronounced "Butt-Head") was the first to tell farmers to "get big or get out." In Butz's view, federal subsidies to American family farmers encouraged inefficient production and created a moral hazard that could best be rectified by diverting these subsidies to Archer Daniel Midlands, Purina, Monsanto, and an assortment of larger consolidated farm operations. Heaven forbid that we might do away with the subsidies all together and find better ways to farm.

Under this regime initiated by Republicans and continued by both parties, smaller family farms grew to be few, the hedgerows were destroyed, topsoil eroded, and gone too are all but the last remnants of the self-sufficient, independent citizenry that once flourished upon the country's agriculture. Of course, the republican society that once flourished on the foundation of widely distributed property with its hallmarks of civility, manners, and hospitality has all but vanished as well. Thus, Gentleman Bob is rarely heard in his former haunts on a June morning.

Guns, Yankees, and Such

The antipathy of many urbanites who reside in Greater New England (think Old New England and the Midwest) toward firearms and their possessors has always left me puzzled. In addition to editorials and the parade of talking heads preaching the gospel of "gun control," which really amounts to people control, I have come face to face with firearms aversion among some of my wife's kin. And being a "nat'ral born durn'd fool" I have from time to time rushed headlong into the fray to convert the heathen to the gospel according to Remington, Mossberg, and Marlin. Firearms aficionados will recognize that I am low church when it comes to firearms. Placing my face in a running fan, or dashing my head against a brick wall, or spitting in the wind might have been a more fruitful use of time. After a bit, I decided it was time to withdraw from mission work and seek to understand my kin-in-law's unregenerate, unenlightened, and superstitious stance on firearms.

So how come so many "damn Yankees" (though not all) hate and fear guns? First it is important to be clear about who and what a Yankee is. Long after the Puritans lost their faith, they and their descendants have maintained, at least in their own minds, their status as the elect. Suffice to say, the Yankee, or secular Puritan if you prefer, has replaced whatever faith he had in God with faith in himself and his world view, no matter how at odds it may be with truth and reality. Now, all Yankees are Northerners, but not every Northerner is a Yankee. Yankees are usually found in the academy, large global corporations, politics of course, and any other field where there is the possibility of rooting up freedom and happiness. Indeed, Northern non Yankees deserve our admiration and respect for having to put up with Yankees for much longer and in much closer proximity than Southerners until very recent times. Wannabe Southern Yankees are known as scalawags. Now that we have that out of the way ...

In the past I fought against the darkness of ignorance by supplying my opponents with a plethora of data, and data a plenty there is. A Pew Foundation study found that firearm homicides peaked in 1993 and by 2010 had trended 49% lower. Likewise, non-fatal incidents with firearms also dropped by 75% during the same period. The Department of Justice found a similar drop in firearms homicides and non-fatal firearms incidents for the same period (a 39% drop and 69% drop respectively). What about all those school shootings you ask? Well, the National Council on Educational Statistics found similar falling trends with respect to violence in schools. After peaking in 2006, violent incidents at school dropped to an eighteen year low by 2010. Likewise, non-fatal school violence has been trending down since its peak in 1993. Even on a global basis the United States comes off well. Nowhere else is gun ownership higher than in the United States, yet the United States ranks below the global mean and median for total homicides (Crime Prevention Research Center, 2014). All of this occurred even as the number of firearms in private hands across the United States soared to 310 million.

Child safety advocates have consistently argued that the presence of firearms in the home presents an unacceptable risk to children, since accidents do happen. Well, not according to the Centers for Disease Control. In 2007, the CDC found that automobiles, drowning, fire, and suffocation were far greater risks to the lives and health of children than firearms. Drilling down a bit on drowning deaths of children, one finds that 75% of accidental drownings of children occurred in pools. Put another way, in 2007 more than 450 children died in pools because of accidental drowning, meanwhile a total of 124 children died from a firearms accident. I have yet to see child advocates call for the banning of swimming pools and automobiles—I suppose the mortality rates among children from these are acceptable risks, as well as an acceptable cost of the American Dream.

What we do know from all these studies over the last few decades is two things: widespread gun ownership does not *per se* create a more violent society or an unacceptable risk to children or adults and that in a society where there is widespread gun ownership, the weapon of choice to do someone in will be a firearm, more accurately a handgun. Does this mean that if we get rid of firearms the homicide rate will trend even lower? Not necessarily, the United Kingdom, according to Home Office crime statistics, experienced a spike in homicides after their gun ban was imposed (The trend has since come down to pre-gun ban levels.) And while a handgun is easy to operate, a Louisville Slugger is even more so. The advocates for banning guns also focus their ire upon semi-automatic versions of rifles that sport an AR-15 or other military platform. Yet these firearms account for fewer homicides than knives and blunt instruments (FBI Uniform Crime Report, any year). Anyone with a modicum of gun sense knows that the iconic bolt action deer rifle is built upon the military rifle platforms of World War One, but as Senator Dianne Feinstein once pointed out, the AR-15 looks "scary."

So, what is really going on here? Why does the debate over guns remain heated and passionate and immune to reason? The reason, I believe, is that the debate is fundamentally cultural. Allow me to explain. I asked my wife about her many extended kin from the deep North, and why they did not agitate for the banning of swimming pools since these represented a far greater risk of accidental death than firearms (My apologies to all y'all who have formed the City on the Hill Central Committee for Keeping Our Children Safe From Rogue Drownings by Swimming Pools). My wife kindly replied, "It's simple dear; they would tell you that the only thing a gun was made for was to kill people." My cool and rational rejoinder was, "So what?" Now the reality is that firearms do have other purposes, and I know that far more ammo is expended in target shooting than in hunting and homicides combined. But the view of my kin-in-law, and my response, does suggest a provocative cross regional analysis is in order.

I do believe that when the average Yankee urbanite (Yubbies) sees a firearm their visceral reaction is to see, *ipso facto*, an instrument of chaos, disorder, and bodily harm. The Yubbie, whether he is aware of it or not, is the inheritor of a tradition that views government as the entity that keeps the darkness at bay, and his rights intact. It is the passions of the individual which must be curbed and brought into order, for without order, no liberty is possible. When Mr. Obama chided rural voters for wishing to "cling to their Bibles and their guns" he gave perfect voice to this sentiment. The Bible is a passé and dated for the new swinging paganism, and guns, well fools don't you know the government is trying to protect you from such things, and the people that wield them? What is most interesting is the Greater New England habit of finding evil in instruments rather than in acting moral agents, unless you happen to be Southern. Yubbies have been in the forefront of the crusades against alcohol, cigarettes, and firearms, because all of these represent an instrumental threat to the progressive order they champion. And my dear reader, whether you wish it or not, that progressive order includes you!

Now your average Southerner does not view the world in the same way. Disorder, though it can be a problem, is best handled and regulated at the local level. This is merely an expression of the old idea that all justice is personal. The greatest danger for an old timey Southerner is the perennial human lust for dominion and power. Old timey Southerners have always been distrustful of BIG, be it big government, big money, or big corporations, which really are all the same thing— they go together like love and marriage, horse, and carriage. Moreover, the old timey Southerner loves the old constitution, but he knows it is a paper barrier. So guns make sense to him. They afford protection from the local disorders that may afflict him and those he must defend (think home invasion), and they serve as a counterweight against BIG. The poor Yankee urbanite has his sleep disturbed by the mere thought that there are over 300 million firearms in the hands of private citizens; the old timey Southerner sleeps better for it.

Thus, dear reader, we will never really see the end of the gun debate. Most Southerners of my acquaintance really do not care if Massachusetts bans everything from pea shooters to AR 15s, none of them are making plans to move North. Ah, but we know our good Yankee progressive cannot stop at the borders of his home state; he wants to bring the City on the Hill to you, whether you want it or not. On the issue of guns, we are and will remain still Rebels, still Yankees.

Pietas in the Era of Revolution

Pietas, the most Roman of the virtues, refers to the duty every individual owes to one's country, parents, kin, and ancestors. It is from *pietas* that patriotism, not nationalism, springs forth. It is a virtue that was once esteemed by Americans, for once upon a time Americans were formed by the classics of ancient Rome, especially in their political and literary imaginations by the old Roman Republic. This was most true of the South. Well into the twentieth century a student could gain admission into the University of South Carolina by translating selections of works by the ancient Greek and Roman authors. Education concerned itself not with professional training, but with becoming conversant in the great conversation of western civilization. Training in the professions followed the completion of one's education. Tradition, understood as the handing down of the best that had been thought and said, was deeply embedded in both liberal and classical approaches to education. Indeed, such an education taught that the duty to submit to tradition was a grave one. The upholding and transmission of tradition was an act of filial piety toward one's ancestors whose meticulous labor both preserved and built upon the edifices of the past from which we the living were ennobled and enriched. It was a long-standing conservative principle that no one individual or group had a right to judge tradition on their own authority. A tradition might be adjusted via a slow organic process through time, or some traditional practice might be altered that was in direct conflict with divine revelation or the natural law. In those cases where tradition was found wanting it might take generations before the conflicts might be resolved.

The erection of monuments is in part an act of *pietas*, a taking care of the dead. What the monument celebrates is not the deification or canonization of the person whose likeness it represents. The monument calls to mind some virtue or three the person exercised in their lifetime, often to a heroic degree, and is a lesson that such virtues are to be imitated by us their actual or figurative progeny. The monuments erected in honor of specific political and military

25

leaders of the Confederacy and of its ordinary soldiers and citizens, are meant to call to mind the fortitude, forbearance, patience in suffering, and self-sacrifice practiced by these men and women. When the Great Compromise between North and South was still in effect, this truth was understood by all Americans. One did not have to be a partisan of the Gray or the Blue to appreciate the heroic exercise of virtues by those each side, memorialized in granite or bronze. Indeed, this should be the working assumption of any civilized individual who comes upon the monuments of the other side. Only barbarians desecrate.

Let us not forget there was once a tradition in America, especially south of Mason's and Dixon's line, where "small r" republicans eschewed all monuments as an exercise in vanity and a violation of republican simplicity. George Washington was of this mind, so too were the Old Republicans Nathaniel Macon and John Randolph of Roanoke. Macon burned much of his correspondence and personal letters, when Randolph died his marker was fittingly an ancient oak on his property at Roanoke whose roots were entwined with his remains. A later generation removed his body for internment in Richmond's Hollywood Cemetery. What would such men think of the republic today where narcissism and vanity have such a tight grip upon everyone from "celebrities" to the ordinary account holders on various social media platforms? Are such a people worthy or even capable of self-government?

At one time Americans could so pronounce the same judgment upon their enemies, but no more. Since the 1960s we have been living in the age of the perpetual revolution, it is more accurate and fitting to say the age of impiety. The raging mobs of iconoclasts, whose zeal is only exceeded by their ignorance, are more to be pitied than despised. Given the consequences of original sin, piety is not an innate virtue, it must be learned and acquired. And who were the teachers of our current crop of revolutionaries? Why the burners, rioters, and looters of the 1960s, who opted for the Gramscian long march through the churches, the academy, the corporations, and the media. The generations now in power, who brought to us such blessings as abortion, divorce, the exclusion of Christianity from the public square, and a host of "isms" were only capable of passing on to those youth who have been thoroughly radicalized by the Eternal Revolution. Indeed, so many of our "Conservatives," our dear American Girondins, have shown themselves to be half-hearted supporters of half-measures in support of the Eternal Revolution. This support takes the form of pronouncing denunciation and charges of "traitor" and "white supremacist" upon the heroes of the South. And what pray tell then shall we call Washington, Jefferson, Madison, Henry, the Adams family, Hamilton, and the rest who were in the forefront of the effort to win their country's independence from perfidious Albion? The mob in their glee hurls the charge that if one agrees that Calhoun must be canceled, how then does one protect Lincoln given his racial views? The American Girondin is usually at a disadvantage in effectively answering these questions, he is often as ignorant of history and its complexities as his Jacobin antagonist.

As for our impious Jacobin, he is reduced to a violent and dangerous caricature, a figure whose politics are both ironic and insane. The Jacobin decries all forms of bias, racism, sexism, and a host of other isms with relish and glee. He is quick to define the positions of his adversary, protest from the adversary notwithstanding, and put the match to the strawman. Thus, one who is sympathetic to the South is a racist, a defender of traditional marriage or the science of biology is a sexist, transphobe, homophobe, even an "omniphobe" as that should cover all the phobias. These silly stereotypes used as so many "bullets" in a game of invective are a perfect example of the very behaviors our dear Jacobin purportedly opposes. In defense of the "oppressed," the Jacobin becomes a nightmarish oppressor. So often the Jacobin's conclusions in this infantile game of name-calling is counter to reality. Two examples will suffice. The American Jacobin (and the American Girondin) insist the Late Unpleasantness was only about slavery, but we know from the very letters and journals of the people who fought and died in that conflict that this is not so. A host of issues and conditions motivated Billy Yank and Johnny Reb to take up arms. As for the Jacobin charge of "systemic racism," where exactly is the system? Jim Crow, the last system of racism in the United States, died an overdue death a long time ago. And indeed, if systemic racism is so pervasive, how have so many people of African descent risen to such prominent positions of power and influence in politics, entertainment and sports, and the media? Each of these areas of endeavor were and remain crucial in shaping the culture of contemporary America, at least for the present.

What all this demonstrates is that once the impious destroys the ties to tradition and piety, so too are the virtues that allow for civilization to be sundered. The impious, by rejecting the patrimony bequeathed to them, become like the tragic characters populating so many of William Faulkner's novels. Their rejection of tradition leaves them without an identity, without a history, ever seeking utopia, retribution, or both. They are not constrained or masters of themselves, they are enslaved to their emotions and appetites. Society is not a creation of the here, nor the product of mere appetite, it is built upon the achievements, mores, and customs of past generations. One can reject the patrimony, but once the house is pulled down and the Jacobin has sown the wind, what then shall he reap?

Through a Glass Darkly:
Justice Kavanaugh and
the Triumph of Symbol over Reality

> History does not repeat itself, but it often rhymes.
>
> — Attributed to Mark Twain

Americans at their best are a pragmatic "can do" folk, be it "Yankee ingenuity" or good old fashioned "get 'r done." We are at our worst when we stray from this pragmatic bent into the misty fields of sacerdotal ideology, which is to say when we ascribe to our pet ideologies a sacred nature, and confer a sainthood, or at the very least priestly ordination, upon our favored ideologues. In the antebellum period, abolitionist ideology exercised over the course of time a profound effect upon the Yankee mind. More Northerners, even those whom the abolitionists annoyed, came to accept the idiocy of the "slave power conspiracy." For the innocent and uninitiated, this conspiracy theory asserted that Southern slaveholders were planning to use the powers of the federal government to expand slavery into the territories and throughout the Union. Once this was accomplished, free white labor would be degraded, and the stout wheat farmers of the Midwest would find themselves enslaved. This was nonsense.

During the crisis of the 1850s Southerners did insist on being allowed equal access to the territories, which did mean that slaveholders could settle in the territories with their slaves, but everyone knew this was not happening and was not going to happen. There was a bare handful of slaves in the territories; ironically, the anti-slavery, Mormon dominated Utah territory had the most slaves, twenty-nine, according to the 1860 census. Realities, however, no longer mattered. Symbols defined people's views of each other whether one was opposing the "Black Republicans" or the "Slave Power." Thus, Southerners and Northerners, who had a great deal in common, were after Mr. Lincoln's election ready to kill each other.

On balance, the politicians and intellectuals of the North bear the much greater portion of the blame for the repressible conflict. Beginning with the Missouri Compromise and lasting through and after the war, Northern politicians continually painted the South as a part of Dante's *Inferno*. Southern fire-eaters and pro-slavery apologists began to play the same sort of game, but they were very much Johnny-come-latelies; the most extreme pro-slavery folk were viewed by many in the South as a radical and eccentric minority. Also, the South's politicians were asking for a symbolic concession on the territories issue. Which is to say that most Southerners understood that even if the slave property friendly Lecompton constitution was approved by the federal government for the Kansas territory, eventually slavery would be abolished in Kansas as more Northerners than Southerners made their way into the territory. But when the symbolic becomes real, symbolic concessions, such as what the South had been seeking since the days of John C. Calhoun, become in the minds of many Northerners very real and dangerous concessions. And so, to quote Father Abraham, "the war came."

For a time, it was a restrained war, a war waged by people who were on the whole Christian, through the states and a federal government, under most of the provisions, laws, and customs that governed the prosecution of conflicts. As the war progressed, civilized restraints lost their hold upon the war lords of the North. With the exceptions of Kentucky and Maryland, where brother fought brother, and the Missouri—Kansas savage border conflict, the war was mostly a war between the states. In the war's early years, symbol most ardently challenged reality in the frontiers and borders of the Southland, that is where true civil war reigned.

Which brings us to the present day. The controversy surrounding the confirmation of Judge Brett Kavanaugh to the Supreme Court illustrates that left-leaning Americans are once again embracing the symbolic over the real. In my view, some of us on the right and the left had good reasons to oppose Judge Kavanaugh. Judge Kavanaugh is a decent man and a supporter of the second amendment, but he is horribly wrong on many constitutional issues. His support of and involvement in framing the misnamed "Patriot Act" decidedly places him in the anti-fourth and anti-fifth amendment camp. I am not sure if he realizes that there are a ninth and a tenth amendment to the Constitution, and his support for an expansive executive branch is gravely concerning and violates the view of executive power held by most of the framers of the constitution. Left and right, at least those elements committed to the Bill of Rights, have common ground for a united front to oppose Judge Kavanaugh's elevation to the Supreme Court.

The left, however, chose to make a symbol of Kavanaugh that bears no resemblance to the man. Hoping to portray Judge Kavanaugh as dangerous example of white male privilege run amok, the Senate Democrats relied upon a witness, Dr. Christine Blasey Ford, who was unable to provide even the bare minimum of corroboration, not evidence mind you, but simple corroboration, of her claim that Kavanaugh sexually assaulted her thirty-five years ago. Soon others, even less credible than Dr. Ford, came forth from the woodwork alleging even more terrible and criminal behavior on the part of Kavanaugh in his high school and college days. Senate Democrats ran with it, and soon Judge Kavanaugh found himself the new symbol of evil, white male, patriarchy. Senator Susan Collins is spot on when she suggested that Kavanaugh is far more "moderate" than many on the left believe. That does not matter, what matters to the left, with their threats of impeachment, violence, "resistance," etc. is not who Kavanaugh is, but what he symbolizes in their minds. The Democrats have moved beyond the politics of personal destruction to a politics of hate, and in the political climate of hate, symbol will always trump reality.

What the Kavanaugh case illustrates for the larger political and cultural picture is disturbing. The dividing lines in America no longer run along the Mason and Dixon, the Ohio River, and the southern counties of Missouri. The division occurs as a blue archipelago of metropolitan areas in a sea of rural red. It is now a replay of court versus country. If the current trend continues and the left remains committed to the politics of symbol and hate, God forbid, we have an excellent historical example of what it might look like if the left makes good on its threats of violence. The example is America's first true civil war, the brutal conflict in South Carolina during the American Revolution. There were few niceties and a plethora of atrocities fueled by hatred committed by both the patriot and loyalist. As they say, in the low country of that gallant little state, it was not pleasant. Let us pray the same fate does not await us all.

THE BLUNDERING GENERATIONS
AND THE CRISES OF LEGITIMACY

Crises of legitimacy are rarely resolved without resort to violence. The European experience in the seventeenth century is generously populated with such examples: The English Civil War, Le Fronde I and II, The Thirty Years War, The Great Deluge that rocked Eastern Europe and the Polish Commonwealth. Even the Glorious Revolution, that peaceful coup launched by Anglicans and Whigs against James II, was not all that glorious or peaceful in Ireland and Scotland. Violent aftershocks were felt in both countries until the suppression of the '45 on Culloden Moor. Our own history saw two great bloodlettings brought about by a crisis of legitimacy, the War for Independence and the War Between the States. The latter still plays a prominent role in our confused political culture. Today, "conservative" commentators refer to the Southern bid for independence as a treasonous action undertaken to preserve the institution of slavery. At best, this is a gross over-simplification that contributes to a false understanding of the past leading to misdiagnosis of the ills of our dangerous and increasingly violent times.

A certain generation of sober historians from not too long ago regarded the Late Unpleasantness as a terrible and avoidable tragedy. The narrative tells the tale of a blundering generation of politicians who in the 1850s pushed and pitched the union into a horrific and needless conflict whose toll in death and destruction, at least for the South, was like what European countries experienced at the close of the first and second world wars. The blundering generation exploited the issue of slavery for short term political gain at the expense of domestic tranquility. The status of slavery in the territories was the flashpoint, though what was really at stake was the control of the Presidency and the Senate, and the Supreme Court.

In many respects the status of slavery in the territories was a non-issue. Whatever initial numerical advantages Southern settlers favorable to legal protections for slavery gained in Kansas would be inevitably wiped away by the rising tide of Northern migrants into the region. Demography was destiny, and the game of numbers favored the North. In territories such as California and Nebraska, the South did not stand a chance. Popular sovereignty would hold sway and these territories would enter the union as free states. As to the status of slavery in those states where it legally existed, abolitionists themselves were divided. William Lloyd Garrison argued for expelling the slaveholding states from the Union, John Brown and his financiers favored purging by blood via a slave insurrection the institution of slavery from all quarters of the Union, more moderate types favored some or another scheme of gradual emancipation. The fundamental crisis of the Union was not the status of slavery, it was arithmetic. For the first time in its young history a political party, the Republicans, representing only one section of the United States was on the brink of dominating the federal government.

True, the slavery issue was bitterly divisive and gave an opportunity for extremists on both sides of the issue to move their heated rhetoric into the center of public discourse. The racial views of the day compounded the hostilities between North and South. Northerners who declaimed against slavery, except a tiny minority, were absolutely opposed to increasing the numbers of people of African descent in their states. Those "free" African Americans who lived north of the Ohio found themselves under a regime of laws and customs as strict and oppressive as the Jim Crow legislation introduced in the South decades after the war. Southerners in the antebellum era had few qualms about living with and among African Americans slave or free, if African Americans were in a state of political, economic, and social subordination to whites. The Dred Scott decision was viewed with horror by everyone in the North because it suggested that slavery was a legally protected institution nationwide and might result in Southerners migrating to the North with their African slaves. Northerners had opposed Thomas Jefferson's argument for the diffusion of slavery as a means of bringing an end to the institution, but their opposition was based on their bigotry toward people of African descent. Meanwhile, Southerners viewed attacks on slavery as an attempt to undermine what they viewed as a stable social order by potentially releasing African Americans from their subordination. Southerners were also quick to point out what they viewed as the North's hypocrisy on the related issues of slavery and race, be it the Northern versions of Jim Crow or Northern participation in the lucrative slave trade.

The catalyst for division and war was the aftermath of the John Brown raid upon the federal arsenal at Harper's Ferry. The raid itself was tragi-comic. As Dr. Jonathan White's research indicates, the outpouring of material and moral support in the North for both Brown's call for violent insurrection and its adherents deeply disturbed many Southerners who were committed unionists and politically moderate. What Southern fire eaters were unable to do in a decade, the Secret Six, Brown's financiers and co-conspirators, and the Northern intelligentsia accomplished in a matter of months, the secession of most of the Southern states from the Union.

Northern support for John Brown, the election of 1860, and the actions and policies of Mr. Lincoln called into question the legitimacy of the federal government for many Southerners. It brought to life the warnings of John Randolph of Roanoke and John C. Calhoun. If the South were governed by the North, Southern interests, and not just slavery, would be put into the hazard. For Calhoun, one of the dangers to the federal republic's integrity was the rejection of the principle that the union's benefits and burdens were to be shared equally by the states. The Republican Party's motto in 1860 might as well have been that of every other conqueror in history, "Woe to the conquered, spoils to the victor." The Republican Party had no intention of resisting the temptation of indulging their *libido dominandi,* and with John C. Calhoun, Daniel Webster, and Henry Clay removed from the scene after 1850, compromise was impossible. This being the case, Southern states concluded, one by one and often for varied reasons, that the federal government lacked legitimacy. The resort to military force by Mr. Lincoln's government only confirmed the Southern secessionists in their views.

The guns of that war have long since been silenced, slavery has thankfully ceased, and racial bigotry has waned in the succeeding generations, no matter what the "woke" among us believe; we who have more years and experience know better. An older conflict, however, re-emerged. One need only consult an election map broken down by county to see this ancient Anglo-American conflict in colors of red and blue, center versus periphery, court versus country. The great metropolitan cities and suburbs, college towns, the financial centers, the techno-autocrats of the left coast, are arrayed against the small towns and rural counties of America. Neither slavery nor sectionalism nor the two-party system obscures the conflict now. A wide and deep enmity and distrust now separates Americans and reaches its icy hands to divide colleagues, friends, and families. When Donald Trump was elected president in 2016 his legitimacy was immediately rejected by many in the Democrat Party, and some Republicans as well—the famous "Never Trumpers." Signs and slogans declaring, "Not my president" were everywhere in the urbanized districts of the Court Party. Mr. Trump fought long and hard with the Court party elites who attempted to portray him as a puppet of Mr. Putin and the Russians, he "won" in the objective sense as the evidence clearly indicated he and members of his administration were the targets in a flimsy and clumsy coup on the part of the Department of Justice and other elements of the shadow government. Mr. Biden's apparent electoral victory is under intense scrutiny from Mr. Trump's lawyers and a variety of private citizen organizations convinced his organization, in collusion with the overlords of the tech world and state election officials, committed the most egregious act of voter fraud in the history of the United States. The Court party denies this as a matter of course.

Though the evidence from "Russia Gate" supported President Trump's exoneration and justified a slew of criminal indictments of high officials in the Department of Justice and the Federal Bureau of Investigation, it did not matter. In our post rational society, those who decided Mr. Trump was an illegitimate president will not be moved by such petty inconveniences as facts, sworn affidavits, and evidence.

Meanwhile, Mr. Biden's talk of "healing" or perhaps he means "heeling," is comic in the darkest sense. The harsh and damning terms in which Mr. Trump and his supporters were described by him and his allies the last four years have not been forgotten, nor have the calls to incarcerate Trump supporters in "re-education camps." This is dark and dangerous rhetoric, and it betrays a fatal ignorance of the capabilities of Mr. Trump's supporters. Moreover, better evidence for the illegitimacy of Mr. Biden's election exists than that presented against Trump after the 2016 election. Mr.

Biden's famous remark about having the most extensive voter fraud organization in history no longer seems like a mere lapse in cognitive function from a man on the downslope of consciousness. What the Court party did to delegitimize Mr. Trump's presidency in the eyes of millions is now being done by the Country party, with better evidence, greater integrity, and greater skill. It is turning millions of Americans toward questioning the legitimacy of the election and the Biden regime. Even many Democrats now realize their party is no longer the party of the common person, it is the party of Zuckerberg, Goldman Sachs, globalists, the "perfumed princes" of the pentagon and military industrial complex, political hacks, and bureaucrats: the sort of men whom John Randolph once described as worthy of loathing and fear, for they are the citizens of no country.

The great crisis of legitimacy that resulted in the War Between the States proved our country's greatest and bloodiest war. For the states of Maryland and Kentucky, it was a true civil war, where brother fought brother, cousin fought cousin, yet these implacable foes did retain their humanity toward each other, it was a more Christian age. All of America is now Maryland and Kentucky, circa 1860. The difference is the Court and the Country revile each other, and the lessons of the classics and Christianity will not provide restraint, not in a post-Christian and post-rational society. Three of our greatest statesmen: Daniel Webster, Henry Clay, and John C. Calhoun could only forestall the awful conflict. Abraham Lincoln, Jefferson Davis, Alexander Stephens, and Stephen Douglas, all able men to one degree or another, they and the others of their generation blundered the union into a horrible conflict. What are we to make of likes of Joe Biden, Kamala Harris, Janet Yellen, Mitch McConnell, Nancy Pelosi, Mike Lee, William Barr and the vast sea of mediocrities and blackguards inhabiting the foggy bottom swamp upon which the Court party stands? No one can seriously entertain the notion that these people are of the caliber of the Framers, the Great Triumvirate, or the first Blundering Generation. Are they even capable of discerning the mischief their policies and negligence have wrought upon the country, or the deep mistrust they have helped to sow among their countrymen? What shall future generations make of such men and women?

CONTESTED GROUND:
SOUTHERN IDENTITY AND THE SOUTHERN TRADITION

In the popular imagination the South is viewed as a region typified by racism, poverty, and ignorance save a few special islands, such as Chapel Hill and Charlotte, which lay in the archipelago of enlightenment. There are some cracks in this edifice of Yankee bigotry, but when political and cultural wars become heated, the edifice is trotted out once more to remind the American people as to who wears the white hats and who wears black. None of this, of course, conforms to the far more complex reality from which Southern culture and identity emerged.

Before examining the commonalities that give coherence to the South, it is crucial to understand the important realities of ethnic and cultural diversity that have always been a hallmark of the region. Of the eleven American nations scholars have identified, five are in the South: the Tidewater, Greater Appalachia, the Deep South, New France, El Norte, and the Spanish Caribbean. There is not one Southern accent, but at least eleven different regional dialects. The South is also home to at least five major culinary traditions. There is no doubt that the peoples of the British Isles have left the deepest cultural imprint upon the South, but crucial contributions to Southern culture and tradition have also been made by people of African, German, French, and Spanish descent. Here is true diversity, not the current pretend variety where a community celebrates differences, if everyone thinks and acts within a rigid ideological template.

Important commonalities have also shaped Southern culture and the Southern tradition. The South was until recently an agrarian society. The dispersed settlement patterns found in the South, as well as important cultural practices brought over from the South and West of England, elevated hospitality, and manners to an exalted place in Southern society. For many generations Southerners, both Protestant and Catholic, adhered to what Richard Weaver referred to as the "older religiousness of the South." This religious mentality of Southerners was characterized by an acceptance of the inscrutability of God's will, the authority of the Scriptures, and a deep religious sentiment. In the political realm from Delaware to Texas, most Southerners proclaimed their loyalty to the traditions and practices of political restraint, states' rights, and local governance. One cannot discount the impact of race slavery upon the South, nor the later Jim Crow regime the South adopted from Northern examples. Most crucial, and too often underplayed in the formation of Southern identity, is the experience of secession, war, defeat, and reconstruction, which has among other things, left the South with a legacy of poverty and a deep sense of inferiority. These commonalities are weakening, even as regional dialects and identities are strengthening elsewhere in America; Southern identity and the Southern tradition is slowly eroding.

Before the South entered the crucible of war in 1860, the presence of a unique and coherent Southern identity was doubtful. This is not to say that both Southerners and Northerners recognized important cultural differences between the regions. Moreover, the Southern states gradually became aware of their growing status as a political minority during the antebellum period. Of the solid South that was definitively established in the wake of Reconstruction, however, little was seen until the emergence of the Republican party in the 1850s. The truly national parties had strong footholds in the region, and minus a few important dissenting voices, it was Southerners who embraced the great national wars against Great Britain in 1812 and Mexico in the 1840s. Southerners of the highest caliber embraced the concepts of national greatness and manifest destiny. Henry Clay was in the forefront of this movement as an important leader of the Whigs, and the formidable John C. Calhoun viewed nullification as a remedy to prevent secession—his concern always centered on the right of the South to be treated as an equal partner in the Union. The erratic yet far-sighted John Randolph of Roanoke was often frustrated in his efforts to forge a unified Southern coalition in opposition to the encroachments and consolidation of federal power. He was not above playing the slave card to do so, but even here he hoped to ignite a fear of federal interference in what Southerners considered a domestic matter. The overt defense of slavery as an institution would come in another day by a small minority reacting to what they perceived to be intolerable provocation from abolitionists.

The election of 1860 changed all. The Republican victory was the victory of a regional party, not a national party. The Republicans had controlled the House since 1856, won control of the presidency in 1860, and made inroads into the Democrat's majority in the Senate. The writing was on the wall and so the states of the South began to leave the Union. It was the forge of war, defeat, and Reconstruction that fashioned the "Solid South." Henry Timrod's poem, "Ethnogenesis," captured the situation quite well—the South now had a national consciousness. As a nation, the South underwent the harrowing experience of war, including war made upon its non-combatant population, and in the wake of the war, military occupation, racial animosity, violence, disenfranchisement, and crushing poverty. No state in the old Confederacy was immune from these effects of war and defeat.

The common experience of the South did not end with demise of Reconstruction. The South made a conscious decision not to continue resistance through a guerrilla war, there was to be no "long war" strategy such as the Irish, Poles, and Spaniards pursued in their national struggles. The implementation of dual federalism also defused a renewal or continuation of the conflict. Under this policy, the states and federal government were deemed to have separate spheres of authority and activity, granting to all the states considerable autonomy in their social and economic policies. Booker T Washington's, "Atlanta compromise" speech set down the parameters for race relations in the South. African-Americans would defer their demands for political and social equality in return for Southern white support of Southern black educational and entrepreneurial endeavors. On the cultural front, a great compromise was forged whereby the South was allowed to praise and honor her war heroes if they conceded that the war's outcome was for the best and part of the higher destiny to which the United States was called. Nevertheless, there was an important social and cultural occupation of the South. The South's education system, which before the war was a diverse mixture of public and private academies and colleges, tutors, and for some education abroad, was now modeled upon the public education system of New England. Missionaries from the North came down into the South during the early twentieth century and introduced Fundamentalism in Southern churches. The South which was once the center of horse racing, hunting, and fishing over time adopted the games of its erstwhile enemy: football, basketball, and baseball. True, the South baptized these sports with the appropriate pageantry and ceremony, but it was a significant departure from the region's traditional recreational pursuits. The promoters of the New South worked toward transforming the region economically, taking the North's industrial system as their model.

The great compromise began to crack in the 1920s with the infamous Scopes "Monkey Trial." In a piece published by the New York *Evening Mail* in 1917, H. L. Mencken, the acerbic columnist for the *Baltimore Sun*, portrayed the South in his essay, "The Sahara of the Bozart," as a benighted land, sterile as a desert, given the absence of any intellectual or artistic life. Mencken continued the assault through the 1920s. When Southerners responded to Mencken and other critics of the South, charges were hurled back at the South's heightened sensitivity to well-deserved criticism. The true Achilles heel of the South was not Southern culture per se, but the practice of Jim Crow. True, Jim Crow was nothing more than the codification of informal Northern practices of racial segregation, but the restriction of tax paying members of the community to separate public facilities was grating on any sense of fairness or justice. Contra the decision in *Plessy v. Ferguson*, the separate facilities for blacks and whites were not "equal" by any real measure of quality or quantity. If the NAACP had chosen to attack Jim Crow on these grounds, it is doubtful that Southern states would have been able to afford the necessary upgrades to African-American public facilities to meet the test set down by the decision in *Plessy*. As a result, integration may have occurred under quite different circumstances. Instead, the NAACP and other civil rights organizations chose to attack segregation on the ground of ideology, where a bigoted South must be brought to embrace the primary American principle of equality. The narrative of the civil rights movement became one in which a second reconstruction of the South was justified so that the principle of equality might vanquish the dark forces of racism and bigotry.

Even though the reign of Jim Crow ended in the South, and a much more peaceful end than in many northern states, the demonization of the South was only beginning. As the more socially and religiously conservative region of the union, the South came under regular attacks for its commitment to school prayer and public religious displays, for the defense of the traditional form of marriage, and for any display of Confederate symbols or any sorts of public honors paid to Confederate heroes. These attacks on Southern tradition and culture revealed a good deal more about the second generation of Reconstructionists than they did about the shortcomings of the South. Many of these new Reconstructionists were the inheritors of a secular Puritan legacy and the disciples of cultural Marxism; they began to dominate the academy in the 1960s.

The ideological legacy of the Northern victory in the War Between the States was the triumph of a secularized Puritan ideology. This ideology viewed the United States as nation with a special destiny in history to create a secular city upon the hill which all nations would come to emulate. Robert Penn Warren observed that the War Between the States had conferred upon the South the myth of the "Great Alibi, by which all the region's shortcomings could be laid at the foot of the war. Meanwhile, "the Northerner, with his Treasury of Virtue, feels redeemed by history, automatically redeemed. He has ... an indulgence, a plenary indulgence, for all sins past, present, and future, freely given by the hand of history." This plenary indulgence meant that the Left and other enemies of the South would never be content with mere cultural hegemony, rather they wished everyone to think exactly as they did. When married to cultural Marxism in the 1960s, the secular Puritan mentality viewed identity politics as central to the achievement of a just nation which practiced tolerance, acceptance, and equality. In the name of these new values began the long march through the institutions of education, the arts, media, and government. The new speak of this movement was political correctness, an attempt to seize control of the narrative by seizing control of the language. The new slogan of equality, tolerance, and acceptance became a means of virtue signaling, whereby one could identify with the new moral *zeitgeist*, while excluding those who disagreed with the definition or application of the terms of the new slogan. To accept the Left's meaning and use of the terms equality, tolerance, and acceptance meant to be welcomed into the "big tent" of moral righteousness; to reject the same was to be branded an outcast.

In this matter, many Southerners were only too happy to oblige their moral betters. Thus emerged the self-loathing leftist Southerner who was all too willing to believe and identify with any negative stereotype hurled at Southerners. If this meant that the great compromise was to be repealed so be it. If this meant accepting the Neo-Abolitionist and New Left narratives concerning the Civil War, then so be it. If this meant the destruction of Confederate monuments, then so be it. Indeed, if it meant the reconstruction of all Southern memory, meaning, and tradition, ante-bellum, bellum, and post-bellum, then so be it. These folks became the "Good Southerner" the equivalent of the "Good Indian." The plight of both is similar. No matter how high both rise on the ladder of "civilization," no matter how obsequious each is to their masters, they both remain the unredeemed children of the wilderness. The "Good Southerner" may personally profit by adopting the values and worldview of the enemy of his region, but the payment received for this is the distortion of his history, his culture, and his identity. What is most pathetic and sinister about this situation is the welcome he extends to his own alienation from his true identity and history; indeed, he views his alienation as a sign of redemption. He no longer remembers who he is and is happy for it. When he meets non Southerners or travels outside the region and is asked if he plans to marry his first cousins, he is incapable of even recognizing the attack upon the honor of himself and his people, for he has no honor left. Instead, he embraces the bigotry of his "moral superiors," which is the last accepted prejudice.

Signs of hope do exist. Leviathan is in crisis across the globe. The British exit from the European Union, the rise of Marine Le Pen, the emergence of vigorous nationalist parties throughout the world, and the awakening of secessionist sentiment in California all point toward political devolution. A large factor in this polar shift of global politics is the rise of an alternative digital media that is both nimble and proving difficult to control. The Left also made a grave political error. Unable and unwilling to tolerate any dissent from their social and cultural agenda, they revived a politics of identity that is for them a two-edged sword, a means of division. Given the crisis of legitimacy haunting the country's elites, the electoral fortunes of the Left are not secure, the culture war is not over and done. Less dramatic, but no less significant, is the re-emergence of localism across the political spectrum. Businesses and farms oriented toward local needs and tastes, talented apologists for localism across the political spectrum all give hope of a return to the values of live and let live—and the silencing of the gnostic desire to build universal kingdoms across the globe.

The above unlooked for trends do provide room for a revival of the best in the Southern tradition. The reappearance of the little platoons of society in the form of homeschooling, micro farms, local businesses for local communities, are as welcome as a cool rain in July, may all such thrive and do good in their communities. And we pray of course for a return to the older religiousness of the South, the bedrock of any lasting revival of the Southern tradition.

The South will survive because in many ways it has embodied so much that is good in the Western and Christian traditions. *Contra* our misguided foes, no one is foolish enough to wish for the return of slavery, Jim Crow, or the endemic violence that plagued the frontier regions of the South. What does need to be revived is the traditional Southern respect for nature, the acknowledgement of the inscrutable will of God, the right of local communities and states to govern themselves, and tolerance for those who may think differently from ourselves. A putting away of duplicity, always a mark of the conquered, and an embrace of forthrightness, hospitality, and good manners would go far in healing the region of its real wounds. Most importantly, let us be done with "New South" imitations of modern Yankee businesses, Yankee universities, Yankee education systems, Yankee politics, and Yankee manners. These may have their place, but that place is not here. Let us instead advocate for the best in the Southern tradition and rebuild it each day and in every moment of our lives. Let us avoid (and forgive) the sins of our fathers, but more so let us imitate their virtues and always defend their honor.

The Sins of Harper Lee

A Review of *Go Set a Watchman* (New York, Harper Collins, 2015)

Harper Lee betrayed the literary establishment and many of her readers with the recent publication of her novel, *Go Set a Watchman*. The novel was originally written before the acclaimed, *To Kill a Mockingbird* and when it was published last year the literary public, readers and critics, were most impatient to read it. Many of them had reactions ranging from disappointment to horror. Miss Lee's treason was founded upon literary ambition, and I might add a good literary ambition; the desire to write a novel about a young woman coming to terms with the real world of moral complexity— no Puritan or Manichaean can ever forgive such insolence. And since many of the genus *boobus americanus* carry with them the old Puritan gene, well Harper Lee was doomed.

The charm of *To Kill a Mockingbird* is found in Miss Lee's considerable skill at showing us the world through a child's eyes, and in so doing she gave to American literature the charming figure of Jean Louise Finch, better known as Scout, and the iconic figure of her father Atticus Finch. Atticus is the local attorney in Maycomb, Alabama who takes on the criminal defense of Tom Robinson, an African-American wrongly accused of raping a white woman. Many readers fell in love with the character of Atticus because he seemed to be a Southern liberal facing down the ignorant and benighted racists of Maycomb. The novel's real power was its exploration of the themes of justice and fortitude. As Scout was awakening to the wider world around her, she, like all youngsters, gravitates to the virtue of justice and is an admirer of the virtue of fortitude. Both of these she finds in her father Atticus who is willing to defend the innocent at a considerable social cost and threats to his physical person. Justice and fortitude are the virtues most closely related to sentiment, which is to say we can feel injustice and desire to rectify it, and we can be inspired by fortitude and wish to imitate it. So as

Atticus is to Tom Robinson, so Scout is to Boo Radley. It is a good story, and one that all readers, but especially sentimental readers and critics readily embraced.

The novelist aspiring to greatness, however, attempts more. In *Go Set a Watchman,* Miss Lee attempted to explore the operation of prudence and temperance in the more morally complex world of the South in the 1950s. Scout, now grown up to be Miss Jean Louise Finch, has come home from New York City for her annual summer visit. Maycomb is caught up in the throes of the Civil Rights Revolution (not my term but that of such prominent Civil Rights leaders as Wyatt Walker and Alan Morrison), the town has become less tolerant, more suspicious, and deeply divided along racial lines. Some might argue that once Maycomb's racial order was challenged, the thin veneer of Southern politeness dissolved, revealing the ugly inner racism lurking beneath. Our author suggests in her story that this is a simplistic assertion and shows herself to be neither a Puritan or Manichaean. Indeed, the ability of her protagonist to come into full adulthood depends upon the rejection of a dualistic world view and an appreciation of the moral complexity of her home, and the necessity of prudence and temperance to navigate this world.

Jean Louise's iconic worship of her father as the paragon of justice and fortitude is challenged when she is confronted with two facts about his life: Atticus was once a member of the Ku Klux Klan and he is a current member of the local citizens' council who opposed both desegregation and the granting of voting rights to African Americans. Jean Louise is indignant and distressed by these revelations. Readers and critics joined Miss Jean Louise in her disappointment and distress at Atticus's transgressions. Given the provocative nature of Atticus's affiliations, one might excuse the reaction of both Miss Finch and the critics. Miss Finch feels betrayed, and so do the critics, who are quite convinced that this is a novel about race and dog gone but Atticus is on the wrong side this time.

Well, the readers and critics are wrong; Miss Lee's novel is not about race at all, though the racial conflicts of the 1950s serve as a crucial context for the novel; the novel's theme, however, focuses on Jean Louise's struggle to acquire the cardinal virtues necessary to moral navigation. Indeed, Miss Lee tells us so in the very midst of her argument with Atticus, "The Negroes were—*Incidental to the issue in this war … to your private war*." (243) And what pray tell is this "private war" involving Miss Finch? It is the need of the conscience for the virtues of temperance and prudence. "I need a watchman … to draw a line down the middle and say here is this justice and there is that justice and make me understand the difference" (181-182). Justice and fortitude do not enable one to make such distinctions, thus the need for temperance to gently moderate justice and for prudence, the queen of virtues, to consider those singular and particular things that are the real objects of human action. Prudence rejects the Manichaean impulse to impose justice at any cost.

Lee's thematic focus is on solid ground. Jean Louise, whose sense of justice has been violated by her father's allegiances, enters a state of confusion. Regarding her new home of New York she accuses the city of teaching her the black arts of suspicion and hatred. Her home in Maycomb, however, seems to her to have imbibed from the same chalice as the people of the Big Apple. Dr. Jack Finch, Jean Louise's paternal uncle, plays the role of Virgil in guiding her through the purgatory of adult immaturity. The good doctor calls to Jean Louise's mind the history of her region, the Jeffersonian leanings of her family, the moral rectitude of her father in his respect for both the spirit and letter of the law. When Jean Louise confronts her occasional love interest Henry, an orphan that Atticus raised and brought into his law practice, over his involvement in the resistance to the Civil Rights Revolution, Henry's response is one that speaks to both his and Atticus's motivation for their stance on the race issue, "Have you ever considered that men, especially men, must conform to certain demands of the community they live in simply so they can be of service to it?" (230). It is Henry who informs Jean that Atticus joined the Klan to find out who the men were behind the masks— namely his enemies. Atticus's involvement in the local citizens' council is also nuanced; yes, he believes that the African-American citizens are unready to assume positions of leadership and political responsibility in Maycomb and the South, but he is also unwilling to allow this resistance to be led by men such as the racial agitator Grady O'Hanlon, who Jack Finch describes as a "sadist." When Jean has her last dialogue with Jack Finch, he confronts her with a soul searing charge that Jean is a bigot, "What does a bigot do when he meets someone who challenges his opinions? He doesn't give. He stays rigid. Doesn't try to listen, just lashes out" (267). Jean Louise's way to overcome her bigotry lay along the path of humility. "I mean it takes a certain kind of maturity to live in the South these days. You don't have it yet. … You haven't the humbleness of mind" (273).

The novel's flaws are not in the thematic construction, but in its construction of dialogue. Lee's adult dialogue is a bit stiff and at times reads like a down home version of a secularized Methodist minister channeling Plato. Which is to say the novel has a quality that one critic aptly described as "lumpiness." The novel does not resolve well. We are left uncertain that Jean Louise has acquired some measure of temperance or prudence, let alone "humbleness of mind," while at the same time maintaining a principled opposition to Atticus's social and racial views. To what degree has the conscience of Jean Louise been formed by prudence? Too what degree has her desire for justice considered all of the claims and arguments of her family and community? By novel's end we are left unsure about all of this.

What Harper Lee should be applauded for is her awareness of her strength s as a writer. *To Kill a Mocking Bird* showcased her strengths at presenting the world to us through the eyes of youth while leaving out the "lumpy" parts. Miss Lee played to her strengths which is a prudent course. Jean Louise may or may not have acquired some measure of temperance and prudence, but it is clear that Miss Harper Lee in her too brief career as a writer did acquire these most elusive of adult virtues with respect to her craft. Which is why *Go Set a Watchman* may have remained unpublished until just before her death. The novel's theme required more than charm, it needed the attention of a master.

ALL SLAVERY, ALL THE TIME*

*Apologies to Jon White from whom I stole the title for this piece.

Invariably, any discussion regarding the causes of the Late Unpleasantness brings forth the tortured issue of slavery. Back when I was a graduate student in the 1990s, there was still some room, though not much, for a multi-causational interpretation of the War, not so much anymore. Much of the current historical literature tends to equate the South and slavery as one and the same. In the work of such historians as James McPherson and William Freehling, among others, the South is an inverted King Midas whose every touch is tainted with slavery. Some of this is the result of fashion. Many historians who were in graduate school during the 1960s, or who were trained by the same, found the Neo-Abolitionist view of the War and the South captivating. The Civil Rights movement confirmed the view for some that the true cause of the War, the restriction and ultimate abolition of slavery, was still unfinished until African Americans were elevated to a place of full social, political, and economic equality with whites in the United States. For these folks, history was no longer the activity of painstaking reconstruction and comprehension; it was social and political advocacy.

Not every historian has succumbed. Michael Holt, professor emeritus of the University of Virginia and not one to be mistaken for a partisan of the South, found the reasons for the late unpleasantness in the unpleasantness of the antebellum era, as politicians North and South cynically manipulated the slavery issue for their own partisan reasons. A good introduction to Holt's arguments may be found in his book, *The Fate of Their Country*. My own view is that a good semiotic study of the debates in the 1850s is desperately needed to shed some light on the whole affair. Ours is not the only generation that loved a good "sound bite." Terms such as "slave power" and "Black Republican" I suspect are invested with meanings that go well beyond the literal. Some intriguing semiotic studies of the social and political rhetoric of the antebellum period do exist. Two that I have in mind are Anne Norton's, *Alternative Americas* and Susan-Mary Grant's, *North over South*. For that matter, James McPherson's book, *For Cause and Comrades* offers a healthy respite from "all slavery, all the time." Much to McPherson's admitted surprise (and chagrin?) it turns out that nobody, or very few anyway, were bothering to fight The War over slavery. Though McPherson believes that with Southerners it was unmentioned because it was a given. Hmmm...

So why the continued emphasis on "all slavery, all of the time?" I humbly suggest the following. First, the Civil War is still very much a current event; it is too close to us without our taking sides. This may seem like rank foolishness to most Americans for whom last week was ancient history, Spartans, and all. Yet the visceral reactions to words and symbols remain. Most of the iconoclasts across the pond have focused their ire upon the monuments of people who were imperialists or slave traders or supposed to be such. I do not imagine anyone in England gets much worked up over portraits of Charles II, Prince Rupert, or Oliver Cromwell. I may be wrong on this, but I imagine one might stir up a bit more reaction across the pond by proposing to hang a portrait of Michael Collins or Tom Barry in Westminster Hall. The old Irish Troubles, circa 1919, are much closer than the deadly struggles between Roundheads and Cavaliers. Now jump back across the pond to streets named after Confederate generals, Jefferson Davis's portrait in public buildings, or horror of horrors, Confederate battle flags. Add to this a Yankee migration to the South and one gets the picture. Which leads us to the second point. The symbols of the 1850s and 1860s are still very much alive and kicking. Slavery and slave plantations are still invoked by politicians of both parties. We may no longer speak of "border ruffians" and "bushwhackers," but "redneck" and "grits" (The second a term used in toney liberal neighborhoods in north Baltimore for the "rednecks" who live south of the Patapsco River.) mean pretty much the same. "Damn Yankee," still rolls off Southern tongues as well. We even have some differing customs in honoring the dead who fell at Gettysburg. My brother and I visited Gettysburg shortly after the film of the same name was released. There were understandably far more visitors than in previous years. Southern monuments were as usual decorated with flags and flowers, just more so. Meanwhile several Northern monuments were decorated with money, notes and coins, and votive candles, a curious custom that puzzles me to this day. Donald Davidson was right, in many ways we are still Rebels, still Yankees.

On the darker side of things, many Americans, both North and even in the South I must sadly confess, have a nasty habit, picked up from the unfortunate diffusion of Puritan persons and ideas, of viewing the world through Manichean lenses. We are suspicious of complexity; we like white hats and black hats, the elect and the unwashed heathen. And we are damn sure that the Almighty, whoever that may be for a particular soul, has made sacred our hates and prejudices. Why bother with the painstaking work of understanding people as they understand themselves, when it is so much more fun to demonize them and get a warm fuzzy feeling of self-righteousness as well? It might even help one get elected to public office or sell a book.

So, folks it is all slavery all the time. Whether it is John C. Calhoun, Robert E. Lee, Abraham Lincoln, the Republicans wanting to bring back slavery (As Congressman Rangel of New York would have us believe.), or Democrats trying to keep African-Americans on the welfare plantation (Are white folk on welfare slaves on this plantation as well?), it is all slavery all the time. I imagine it will be until we come to terms with the Late Unpleasantness, and it no longer pays as well to play the slave card.

A Society with Slaves

A review of *Slave and Free on Virginia's Eastern Shore* by Kirk Mariner (Onancok, VA: Miona Publications, 2014).

One of the ironies that plague the proponents of the "South is about slavery and slavery is about the South" school of history is the lack of knowledge we possess regarding the everyday lives and social interactions of the majority of black Southerners, slave and free, who lived south of the Mason and Dixon. We are thus left with some illusions regarding slavery rather than the reality of the thing itself as lived by white, black and red, free and slave. The popular imagination tends to associate slavery with vast cotton plantations worked by hundreds of slaves. The experience of most slaves, however, was on small plantations and farms where five to eight slaves resided and worked side by side with their white masters. Historians have relied upon the records in state archives and university libraries which are weighted toward larger plantations, legislation regarding slavery, and state court cases. This "top down approach," as Mr. Mariner terms it, does reveal a great deal about certain aspects of slavery and slave society, but it also distorts. One example of this distortion occurs in Kenneth Stampp's "classic" work on slavery, *The Peculiar Institution*. Stampp relied heavily upon the manuscript collections in Southern archives, the vast majority of which originated from large plantations. This excluded about fifty percent of those slaves who lived on smaller plantations and farms, as well as the ten percent of those slaves who lived in urban areas, and perhaps another five to ten percent of slaves whose labor was rented out. Gene Genovese's, *Roll, Jordan Roll* offered a much needed correction to Stampp's plantation as concentration camp thesis. Genovese found a more complex interaction between slave and master, but Genovese's work also suffered from the same difficulty regarding the narrow range of sources.

As for legal historians who have braved the troubled waters of slave codes in the South, let us say that we find their innocence and naivete charming. I have long suspected that the slave codes adopted by the Southern states, and even some of the court decisions handed down in cases regarding slavery and slaves, had far more bark than bite and were often unenforceable. The society in which we live today is far more legalistic than the Antebellum South; custom and tradition in antebellum times often trumped both law and judicial verdict. Mariner's fine work suggests that this was often the case in the eastern shore Virginia counties of Accomack and Northampton.

What Mr. Mariner in fact has accomplished in his modest book ranks with some of the past work produced by the *Annales* school in France and the Cambridge group in Great Britain. Mariner unapologetically seeks to make known the hidden figures of history at all levels, while avoiding the temptation, for the most part, of imposing contemporary modes of understanding and social values upon the historical actors he is studying. His is a fascinating local history from the "bottom up," surely as good as that produced by such historians as John Demos, who made New England his focal point. Mariner does enjoy the huge advantage of having access to the county records of Northampton, which may be the oldest and most comprehensive in the United States. What Mariner does is to make excellent use of what is available to him to draw a picture of how slavery played out as a legal, social, and cultural institution in small communities on an everyday basis. Most importantly, the slave holders of Accomack and Northampton counties were small planters and farmers, so the implications of Mr. Mariner's book for filling in at least some of the considerable gaps in our knowledge of slavery are intriguing.

Mr. Mariner begins his work on familiar ground already plowed by the likes of Edmund Morgan and T. H. Breen. He accepts the thesis that Virginia in the seventeenth century was a society with slaves, but would slowly develop into a slave society by the middle of the eighteenth century. Yet, even as the legal status of African American slaves became that of chattel, and the liberty of free African Americans came under greater and more onerous legal restriction, the reality was far "less fixed, much more muddled and fluid." For example: slaves received and owned property granted to them by their masters, slaves often were allowed to hire themselves out and keep a portion of the wages, slave resistance was significant in both passive and more violent forms, and segregation was virtually nonexistent. But, dear reader, there is more. To quote Mr. Mariner,

Blacks and whites, slave and free, lived in close proximity, knew each other and dealt with each other on a daily basis. They regularly mingled together, and sailed together. They went to church together, drank together, and celebrated together. They hatched crimes together, and stood together before courts. Not infrequently they lived in the same houses and slept in the same rooms. (15)

And there is still more. African Americans successfully sued for their freedom in the county and magistrate courts. (These findings lend support to the recent findings of Professor DeRosa regarding slave standing and litigation successes in local, county, and state law courts.) The suits became more frequent through the eighteenth century. As a result, Virginia's law makers passed a law requiring all such suits by African Americans to be *in forma pauperis*, that is the plaintiff had to employ local counsel and damages awarded could only total one cent. Nevertheless, the number of such suits increased, and in some cases Mr. Mariner found that the *in forma pauperis* provision was ignored.

Another example concerning the disjuncture between law and lived reality concerned the Act of 1806 in Virginia regarding free blacks. The law required that all slaves manumitted after 1806 to leave the Old Dominion in one year or face re-enslavement. Those slaves manumitted prior to 1806 were required to register this fact with the county clerk. When the law did go into effect, it was rarely enforced on the local level. Indeed, one Jim Outten was re-enslaved under the Act of 1806 and successfully sued his new master to regain his freedom. In other cases where the county court in Accomack county indicted and sold back into slavery free African Americans manumitted post 1806, the sales were in effect paper sales, the free African Americans continued to live as free men. Nevertheless, many free African Americans did leave the eastern shore of Virginia for Maryland and Delaware, suggesting that while truly being re-enslaved was a remote possibility at best, being legally harassed over one's free status was a real threat.

The question as to why the white authorities in Accomack and Northampton counties would either ignore or reluctantly and haphazardly enforce state laws regarding slaves and free African-Americans is intriguing. As usual the answer is complex. For instance, the resistance to expelling free African-Americans was in part due to labor shortages in both counties, and in part due to compassion for the plight of free African-Americans. Another example of the white concern for the plight of African Americans was the purchase by white slaveholders of elderly slaves at estate auctions who were too infirm to work. The purchase price was usually under one dollar, but the care and maintenance of these folks were assumed by the purchasers who could expect a considerable loss on their "investment." Also of interest was the toleration of intermarriage among folks of African, European, and Native American origin in both Accomack and Northampton counties. Interracial marriage was not infrequent in the 1600s, and not unheard of in the 1700s. Even in the 1800s, though legal, social, and cultural opposition among whites had increased, there will still cases of intermarriage among free African Americans and whites on the Eastern Shore.

Racial tensions would increase on the Eastern Shore with Nat Turner's rebellion, and finally deteriorate during and immediately after the Civil War. One could suggest that this was because whites felt their privileged position threatened by these events, and one would be partially right. If, however, a social system begins to break down, no matter what injustices may have been present in it, many of the accommodations that ameliorated those injustices often disappear as well, and folks are left with the lesser angels of their nature to untangle the mess.

Mr. Mariner wrote an excellent local history, and in many ways a courageous book, that deserves a much wider reading. In our day of virtue signaling, he was wise, I suppose, to lodge the obligatory condemnations of slavery, segregation, and inequality. He was wiser still to go where the sources told him to go, and for this he is to be commended. Most importantly his work is an important challenge to all historians of slavery. It is time to make the long trek through the local sources and archives and construct the history of slavery from the bottom up, *a la Annales École*. If the challenge is taken up we may: 1) Recover the important history of most rather than some who were enslaved and the complex web of interactions that characterized societies with slaves. 2) Be darned surprised at what is uncovered as to how the institution of slavery really functioned in the everyday lives of white, black, and red. And thus we may achieve that most elusive of goods in the historical profession, understanding.

John Randolph and the Formation of an American Conservative Persuasion

One of the great issues of American political history is whether an authentic American conservatism exists. This is a crucial question for Southerners, as the South is historically viewed as the most conservative of the regions of the United States. Louis Hartz, a prominent political theorist during the middle of the twentieth century, answered no, American conservatism does not exist. His seminal work, *The Liberal Tradition in America* (1955), viewed the American political landscape as definitively shaped by a Lockean, liberal consensus. According to Hartz, this liberal consensus resulted from the lack of a feudal heritage in America, the vast resources, and vast spaces available to anyone with a mind to escape their geographic locale or their class, and the middle-class origins of most of the Europeans who colonized America. Though Hartz does not mention it, the initial peopling of British North America happened at a time of grave religious, political, and economic strife in the British Isles. The role of the monarchy, the emergence of a modern financial and commercial order, the structure and role of the church and the forms of Christian worship were ferociously contested in the 1600s. With so much turmoil and institutional change in the British Isles, the idea of American as a land of new beginnings with a Lockean clean slate seemed to make sense

Russell Kirk, one of the seminal conservative thinkers of the twentieth century, answered Hartz before Hartz's book was published. A couple of years before Hartz published *The Liberal Tradition*, Russell Kirk published *The Conservative Mind*, wherein Kirk argued for the existence and continuity of a modern Anglo-American conservatism, whose main influence was the British statesman, Edmund Burke. Kirk emphasized the contributions of Anglo-American statesmen and literary figures to the non-ideological defense of a received social and political order. Some evidence for Kirk's scholarly influence may be inferred from the shift in the conversation regarding the place of conservative thought in the American social and political order. Scholars on the left identified what they believed was a paradox operating in American conservative thought. To wit, how could American conservatives embrace free market economics and its "creative destruction," and at the same time hope to preserve anything? As concerns Southern history, the late Gene Genovese wrote the most effective criticism of conservatism along this tack. In his book, *The Slaveholder's Dilemma*, Genovese argued that Southern slaveholders were caught in a dilemma whereby they were defending slavery, a pre-modern institution, and were advocates for freedom, especially in the economic and political realms. While Genovese had considerable respect for the intellectual ability of the South's master class, he remained skeptical concerning the ability of these men to square the circle. Whether intended or not, Genovese's argument gave considerable support to Hartz's earlier conclusions that the American political order was and is liberal.

Two deeply flawed assumptions were embedded in what we might call the Hartz/Genovese thesis. First was the tendency to ignore or downplay the successful transmission by the early settlers of British North America of their political, social, and cultural institutions and practices. No matter the tumult they were fleeing, the first settlers were intentional in their attempts to replicate and imitate in the new world what had been left behind in the old, and often with remarkable success. The second flawed assumption was to equate capitalism with the free market. Capitalism, defined as behavior where a person deploys capital with the purpose of realizing a profit, certainly does exist in free markets, but it can also exist in other political and economic systems as well. It existed in the late feudal/early modern period as the activities of French textile magnate Jacques Coeur and the powerful Fugger family's international finance enterprises suggest. It flourished under various forms of mercantilism, social democracy, and even today in the officially communist states of China and Vietnam.

Studies of capitalism devote copious amounts of ink to the profit motive, as they should, but little to the risk management activities of capitalists undertaken by the state on behalf of capitalists. Such practices as tariffs, subsidies, state granted monopolies, banker bailouts, government contracts, tax exemptions, publicly financed infrastructure, and liability exemptions, are all examples of risk management undertaken by the state throughout the history of capitalism to benefit certain private enterprises, often at the direct expense of taxpayers and those enterprises not so favored by the government. This suggests that risk management is as important as the profit motive in capitalist societies, and that capitalists are quite at home with rent-seeking and risk management activities undertaken at public expense, and less at ease with the risks and vagaries of free markets.

Indeed, we might posit that the owners of substantial amounts of physical and financial capital seem to prefer cozy relationships with the state to the hurly-burly of a free market. The reasons for this is simple. Deploying copious amounts of capital entails enormous amounts of risk, thus the larger capitalists have the greater temptation to turn to the state. State supported enterprises are large and their effects go beyond the economic realm. Political and social transformations result from these practices; so much of the "creative destruction" in a capitalist economy results from the partnership of consolidated capital united to consolidated government, not the free market. Actual free markets with their concomitant risks often result in more modest and cautious investment activity. United States history illustrates well the snowball effect involved in the marriage of large capital and large government. In the post-bellum era, corporations and financial institutions have grown exponentially in size and power, but so too have both the federal and state governments, and massive social and cultural changes. All of this suggests that the union of large capital with large government is a powerful force for radical changes in society, and that the presence of risk in free markets suggests that free markets and free societies can be ordered to the conservative end of the preservation of a received political and social order.

John Randolph of Roanoke, one of the great exponents of the Southern political tradition, was certainly one who believed that liberty was a bulwark against the creative destruction of what one might call state sponsored capitalism. On the surface, Randolph seems to embody the Southern conservative paradox identified by

Genovese: a socially conservative slaveholder who was also a great advocate for economic liberalism and limited government. A closer view reveals the method in Randolph's madness.

Richard Weaver once describe John Randolph's view of individualism as "social bond individualism." This species of individualism recognized that the rights of the individual are secured within a "social context." It is the "social bond" that is of most interest. In his speech on retrenchment and reform, speaking of the relationship between him and his constituents, Randolph used familial language,

> When I was first honored with their confidence, I was a very young man, and my constituents stood in an almost parental relation to me, and I received from them the indulgence of a beloved son. But the old patriarchs of that day have been gathered to their fathers .... I now stand to them, in *loco parentis*, in the place of a father, and receive from them a truly filial reverence and regard. Yes sir, they are my children ... .

Not only did Randolph speak this way, but so did other Virginians. After debating Patrick Henry in his first campaign for political office, Henry called Randolph aside and said to him, "You call me Father. My son, I have somewhat to say unto thee ... keep justice, keep truth, and you will live to think differently." Henry not only called Randolph "son," Henry used the form of familial address when speaking to Randolph. Yes, Virginia was republican, agrarian, slaveholding, socially and racially stratified, and paternalistic, but many of its leadership class viewed Virginia as a family. In a real sense there was a good deal of truth to this conception, as so many of the old families of tidewater and piedmont Virginia and Maryland were related by blood and marriage. The law in Virginia treated patricide not as murder, but as treason. There is something here of the old Roman way, not surprising as the literate people of Randolph's time were educated in the old Latin classics and looked to Rome for model of statesmanship. Part of that inheritance reinforced the Virginia prejudice that the power of the state had very real limits, one of those limits being the threshold of one's home.

Given Randolph's familial and paternal view of Virginia society, his support of the practice of entailing estates to the eldest son is not surprising. The practice of entails was not required by Virginia law; it was not unheard of an estate being entailed to a daughter. Nevertheless, both Thomas Jefferson and George Wythe advocated the abolition of these voluntary entails in the hopes of achieving their vision of a commonwealth of small farmers through the forced division of great estates. Randolph viewed Jefferson's and Wythe's perspective as abstract social engineering, to use a modern term, and short-sighted in its effects. Entails had advantages. Estates in Virginia that were entailed could not be confiscated for the payment of debts. Land in Virginia equated to political power, and the assault on entails would weaken all landholders by undermining the connection between land and political power. If landed property was diluted and divided, the rise of other forms of property seeking political power became a real threat to the existing order. Landed property was jealous of liberty, suspicious of energetic government, and concerned with the preservation of good order. Other forms of property were not so inclined. Indeed, the electoral reform proposed at the Virginia Convention in 1829-30 would have shifted the qualification for voting from landholding to a minimum payment of taxes, the effect of which would disenfranchise poorer freeholders. Randolph argued strenuously against the proposal. Speaking of merchants and manufacturers seeking tariff protection in the years after the War of 1812, Randolph said of the men of capital and finance that he "feared and loathed" those men "for they are the citizens of no place." In his disgust regarding the abolition of entails in Virginia, John Randolph remarked, "Well might old George Mason exclaim that the authors of that law never had a son!"

Randolph possessed a unique insight into the nature of the relationship between property and power. Any attempt to separate power from property, universal suffrage comes to mind, is doomed to failure. As Randolph observed, "the moment you have separated the two, that very moment property will go in search of power and power in search of property." Randolph's fear of the manufacturing class and the banking class was based on this principle. If landed property was separated from power, then the financiers or the owners of physical capital would come to power. In a striking metaphor, Randolph quoting Genesis stated, "'Male and female He created them; and the two sexes do not more certainly, nor by a more unerring law, gravitate to each other, than property and power. You can only cause them to change hands." It was this changing of hands Randolph fought to prevent. The landed gentry had a real and concrete interest in the country, the financier and manufacturer, Randolph's "citizens of no place," the globalists of our own day, do not.

Randolph's familial view of society shaped his view of law and the ability of the law to shape and enforce social norms. In Randolph's view, passing laws to regulate social behaviors was counter-productive, and often had the opposite effect than was intended. He saw custom, tradition, and duty as more effective moral restraints than legislation. In large part, this was due to Randolph's view of people as free moral agents whose behavior was best shaped by customary restraints, as well as familial and social bonds, and powerful social penalties, such as ostracism, that Virginia's local societies could impose. He opposed state laws against public drunkenness because such laws weakened the local community's traditional moral prohibitions. Randolph contended that moving the regulation of public drunkenness into the realm of law resulted in even more instances of the proscribed behavior as the members of society deferred their duties of moral and social regulation to the state.

What was proper to the state of Virginia, or any state government, was the preservation of the received order that had stood the test of time. The duty of the citizen of the commonwealth was to resist any legislative or constitutional changes to the received order, and to grant a broad field to custom and tradition to preserve the received order. As this pertained to Randolph's Virginia, it meant the preservation of the birthright of liberty bequeathed to all free born, free holders of property in the commonwealth. Since Virginia society was familial in its essence, it was also naturally hierarchical as well. Equality was a legal artifice, and no better a legal artifice than the awarding of titles of nobility by legislative or monarchial fiat. The landed gentry exercised power and authority in Randolph's Virginia, holding the crucial political offices of sheriff, justice of the peace, and surveyor; it was customary and traditional that this class hold political power on both the county level and state level. The elevated status of the landed gentry in Virginia came with responsibilities.

Independence, self-sufficiency, mastery of self were expected. In a letter to Thomas Marsh Forman of Maryland, Randolph stated his opposition to the idea of hereditary offices, the gentry of Virginia held their political offices on the tenure of "*Good Behavior.*" Many of these local offices and their duties were brought over from the south and west of England. William Fitzhugh, writing to Ralph Wormley in 1684, described the political offices in Virginia as a "continued usage and practice" of "the laws and customs of England." Those adaptions to the duties and practices associated with these offices, made necessary by the unique conditions of America, only reinforced the prescriptive nature of Virginia's political order.

When significant innovations in the commonwealth's political and social order were proposed at the Virginia State Convention of 1829-30, Randolph opposed them. In particular, he resisted attempts to end freehold suffrage, lifetime tenure for county magistrates, and ending the practice of judicial nominations via the county courts for the popular election of county judges. His reasoning was eminently conservative. The old constitution of 1776 was imperfect, but it served well the commonwealth. The changes proposed would fundamentally alter the old order, Randolph warning that, "Change is not reform." The fountainhead of change was the "lust for innovation," fueled by passion unbridled by virtue, and blind to the unforeseen consequences of setting dangerous precedents for continuous change and turmoil, what has become in our own time perpetual revolution and its hideous attendants, political, social, and cultural degradation.

The change agents of Randolph's Virginia, dangerous though they were, were not the gravest threat faced by the old commonwealth. The federal government held this distinction. Randolph viewed the American political system as an *imperium in imperio*, a system of shared sovereignty between the states and the federal government. The federal government came from the very "breath of the nostrils of the States." The states, in Randolph's view, were not mere political units under a sovereign national government, but unique societies possessing their own distinctive cultures and interests. The federal government was the agent of these sovereign societies for the accomplishment of certain common goods, but at the same time it was also an ominous threat to these unique societies. First, the federal government had a lack of "common interest with the governed," so limiting the scope of federal authority was crucial to curbing tyranny. If once these limits were crossed, Randolph believed there was no turning back. Second, the evil of loose construction, or in a more specious form of cant, the "living constitution," set loose what Randolph called "vagrant powers" in search of some clause of the constitution to which they might attach themselves. Drawing upon his antifederalist heritage, Randolph decried the elasticities in the commerce clause, the supremacy clause, and the general welfare clause that lend themselves as most effective tools to the aggrandizers of federal power. Since the constitution was not prescriptive but positive, its abstract nostrums merely required interpretation to justify plunder and tyranny, with the power of the positive law as the basis for the usurpation of state and local prerogatives and rights. Randolph once said of written constitutions in a speech, "I have no faith in parchment sir, I have no faith in the abracadabra of the Constitution."

To preserve the integrity of the various states, minimal and limited government was necessary. Randolph's actions as a congressman, his speeches, and his letters demonstrate that he was among our most consistent statesmen championing limited government. Randolph opposed protective tariffs because they plundered one section of the country, the South, for the benefit of the other sections. Randolph opposed standing armies because of the direct threat to liberty they always pose, and because of the armies of contractors and lobbyists they brought in their wake. He detested the national banks because he knew them to be the bed where the marriage of government and creditor was consummated, and the citizens disinherited. If the old order of the American states was to be preserved, then the free market must reign. The manufacturers would have to find someone else other than the taxpayer to underwrite their risks. The bond financiers would be banished from the temple, there being no public debt to purchase, and consequently no influence over the counsels of the country, and no taxpayer to underwrite the public creditor's risks. A federal government where the power of the sword and purse were limited meant the states would be left alone, a masterly inactivity would reign in government, and political objects at rest would be allowed to remain at rest. This was Randolph's stated wish, and it is eminently conservative. Such was not to be, let us not, however, lay the blame at the feet of the free market. Randolph well understood the old adage that capital is timid, and in its timidity, capital would seek to unite itself to political power to control its risks and achieve its ends. The recent financial history of the United States is a powerful testament to this fact. Land has long since been abandoned by power, but let us have no nonsense, the "people" have not taken its place. As Randolph observed, property and power seek each other out; it is financial capital that now rules the day, and it is not a conservative power. Large government, the standing military, and large capital have been engines for massive political, social, and cultural change in these Unite States since the surrender at Appomattox. Financial capital married to consolidated political power, the great evil hatched by the adversary, Alexander Hamilton, is the primary temporal source of chaos in the American polity. Authentic Southern conservatives have fought valiantly through history against this hideous strength, recalling by their actions the teaching of Randolph, "Change is not reform!" Nor is it conservative.

Poison Under the Wings:
The Constitution and Its Defects

The beginning of the American political order goes much further back than the Philadelphia Convention of 1787. Political scientists and political theorists are understandably fixated on the Constitution and the convention that produced it. Eric Voegelin, Willmoore Kendall, and a few others go even further back searching for a continuity in the political symbolization present in some certain select, but not all, American political documents of the colonial era. Origins and foundings are broader and more complex things than a selection of documents or the deliberations that one constitution convention can reveal. Any political order is bound up with the cultural, religious, social, and political *ethos* and *eidos* of a people and their society. In the American experience, there was not one founding but thirteen and these "foundings" took place over a period of slightly more than a century. Present in these thirteen political orders were powerful commonalities and significant differences among each of the thirteen distinct societies. What is the most significant cooperative action on the part of these thirteen states, the War for Independence, was as much a source of division as it was of unity. All the colonial governments seceded from the British Empire, but only a minority of colonists, one-third if we believe Mr. John Adams, perhaps as low as one-fifth if some scholars are to be believed, favored secession from Great Britain. A plurality just wanted the war to go away. Of course, this is not important, unless one is in the habit of introducing your constitution with the phrase, "We the People ...."

The story of the American political order, at least to this point, is the collapse of the influence and autonomy of the local into a consolidated political and financial order, what Thomas Jefferson's people called monarchy. This order is not merely political, it includes cultural, social, religious, and political mores and habits national in their scope and often emanating from institutions closely aligned with the centers of political and economic power. American values and views regarding marriage and family were profoundly and quickly changed by the entertainment produced in Hollywood, financed by Wall Street, and regulated by the politicians and civil servants in Washington, D. C. What we have now is an American imperial order under enormous strain from both external and internal pressures. This American imperial order experienced a meteoric rise after Appomattox and is now undergoing a similarly fast meteoric decline. The symptoms are there for all to see. We have not decisively won an armed conflict since World War Two, we have been bogged down in endless conflicts on the peripheral parts of the American zone of hegemony and resource extraction. The national political conflicts have acquired a tone of stridency incompatible with republican compromise. In Washington, D. C., the conflicts between President Trump and his enemies are really about nothing more than who will hold power and enjoy its privileges. Both President Trump and his adversaries are attempting to preserve a status quo that can no longer be preserved. Trump's status quo is an old-fashioned America flexing its industrial and productive might on the world stage. His opponents, the surveillance state, the legacy media, and the beneficiaries of forever war, are committed to a state of affairs allowing them to aggrandize their own power and wealth no matter the cost to ordinary Americans and their civil liberties, not to mention the poor unfortunates across the globe in the sights of the latest drone strike. If you wish to find a villain, the cartographer of this mad destiny, one need look no further than Alexander Hamilton, who mapped the road to political and financial consolidation. True, Hamilton may recoil in horror at what American has become, but what we now have is the logical outcome of his system.

Some defenders of the constitution will view the current disorder in the American state as a deformation of what the "Founders" had in mind. This raises the question as to what the gentlemen at the Philadelphia Convention had in mind for the new plan of government. This is not as easy to discern as some scholars believe. Take the case of the man reputed to be the "Father of the Constitution," James Madison. Is the Constitution the one explicated by Madison, via the medium *Publius*, in the Federalist Papers? Both Madison and Hamilton argued against the inclusion of a bill of rights in Federalist 39 and Federalist 84, respectively. Hamilton, true to form, thought the whole idea of a bill of rights was "not only unnecessary ... but would even be dangerous." Or perhaps we should look to Madison's comment to a correspondent later in life when he wrote that the true meaning of the constitution was to be derived from the proceedings of the state conventions that ratified the new plan of government. And if we choose this latter path, which state conventions shall we look to for the meaning of the Constitution?

What we do know from the history of the republic is that the *Novus Ordo Seclorum* came out of its cradle a bit wobbly. In the first sixty years of the new union's existence, at least four major constitutional crises threatened an end to the American experiment. The fourth, erroneously referred to as the Civil War, witnessed the grandchildren of the generation who seceded from England filling each other's bodies with lead. Better evidence for the existence of fundamental disagreements regarding the meaning of the Constitution and the nature of the federal union does not exist than the over 600,000 who lay dead on the battlefields. What has become of the *Novus Ordo Seclorum* since Appomattox? In substance, it is a consolidated unitary state where the old state militias were federalized into a national guard, a federal income tax was fixed upon the people, a new central bank with a monopoly on the currency was created, the federal bureaucracy metastasized in both numbers and political power, and the imperial regime of forever war was inaugurated.

Nationalists with a triumphalist bent will argue the necessity and the good of the American imperial regime. They believe there was no other choice present in 1789, the thing needed to be set in motion to achieve something called American greatness. The old Roman question, "Cui bono?" applies here. Were there no other choices in 1789? Crucial situations in the foreign and domestic arenas needed to be addressed. The British had not yet withdrawn from the Northwest as stipulated in the Treaty of Paris. The Spanish denied American shippers the right of deposit in New Orleans. All European nations were reluctant to extend any sort of most favored nation status to the American confederacy. Shay's Rebellion underscored the potential for civil disorder among the unpaid veterans of the recently won war for independence. No doubt, the framework of the confederation needed bolstering and improving. Most Americans in public life believed this was possible if the Congress were given a source of revenue independent of the states, say a five percent *ad valorem* duty on imports. Such a duty could fund a naval force crucial to protecting American commercial interests. Some sort of free trade zone among the members of the confederacy was important to achieve, as was also the framework for a unified foreign policy. The states sending representatives to the Philadelphia Convention had these reforms and issues in mind. The delegates from Delaware, Pennsylvania, Virginia, North Carolina, and New Hampshire were given implicit instructions to modify the Articles of Confederation. The legislatures of Massachusetts, New York, and Maryland were much more explicit in their instructions to do nothing more than modify the Articles. Only the delegates from New Jersey received a blank check to do as they saw fit at the convention. All but the delegates of New Jersey exceeded their authority. The plan for government that came from the Philadelphia convention was what Patrick Henry referred to as a beautiful butterfly with "poison under its wings."

The supremacy clause of the Constitution is a tale of both poison and the operation of the law of unintended consequences. James Madison introduced a motion to give the new national legislature a veto over state laws. The motion met considerable resistance and debate. Luther Martin of Maryland, a committed defender of the rights of states, reached back to the old New Jersey plan for a compromise. Martin proposed that the laws made by Congress and the treaties made and ratified by the new government would be the supreme law of the "respective states, as far as those acts or treaties relate to the said states" and judiciaries of the states were bound by these laws and treaties "in their decisions." The clause as proposed by Martin was unanimously agreed to without dissent at the convention. In later drafts it was altered to further strengthen the hand of the federal government, federal laws and treaties being the "supreme law of the land," and thus became the cornerstone of federal judiciary power. Martin had intended the laws of the federal government to enjoy supremacy only when explicitly contradicted by state law and not to enjoy a supremacy over state constitutions and bills of rights.

The predicament for the defenders of states' rights and local governance is even worse than that caused by the supremacy clause. John Randolph of Roanoke once labeled the Constitution a "paper barrier," easily trespassed upon and violated. Within its confines, any number of clauses can be and have been used to justify the most egregious power grabs. Take your pick: the treaty making clause, the war powers clause, the general welfare clause, or as Randolph warned, all these powers in the aggregate will be invoked to grow the federal leviathan at the expense of the states and the people. If it is true that the Constitution brought forth a governing order not seen since the High Middle Ages, the *imperium in imperio*, it has proven even more correct that the Constitution, in the words of Patrick Henry, "squints at monarchy." The parchment barriers erected against monarchy and consolidation, primarily the separation of powers and the bill of rights, are only as effective as the force which backs them. In this age of the surveillance state, star chamber proceedings and black budgets, and the flouting of any rule of law by our politicians and their financial backers, how is it that Henry was not right?

The constitutional order framed in Philadelphia may well be the result of a great American defect—impatience. At the Virginia state ratifying convention, Patrick Henry pleaded for due time for careful deliberation. It was not forthcoming, and it is significant that the champions of the Constitution, especially Edmund Randolph, made the argument in favor of haste. When the Second War of Independence, the War Between the States, ended in the defeat of the secessionists, what Henry and Randolph envisioned came to pass, an American imperium of consolidated and omnipresent government.

If impatience in part resulted in the defeat of the localists, patience will assure their victory. The Hamiltonian order is not sustainable, we are living through the twilight of the international American imperium, and at home we flirt with domestic and civil unrest. The restoration of the local will begin in the localities of America. It will result from living deeply in the communities where we are situated, from being good neighbors, and engaging in the public affairs of our local neighborhoods, towns, and counties. It requires a secession of the heart from the propaganda and distortions directed at us by Leviathan and its handmaiden, the legacy media, and a turning toward faith, the old virtues: theological, cardinal, and civic, family, tradition, and property. Next to true charity, the willing of the good, it requires patience and a commitment to "the long game." We plant seeds in our time; we will not live to see the harvest—but our affection and charity reaches out to the generations who will benefit from our husbandry. Thus, will the authentic American order be restored.

Zombies No More:

Secession, Nullification, and the Academy

A review of *Nullification and Secession in Modern Constitutional Thought*. Sanford Levinson, ed. Lawrence, KS: University of Kansas Press, 2016.

The undead walk among us still, or so asserts Sanford Levinson, the editor of an important collection of essays on nullification and secession. Levinson and company are as mainstream a group political scientists, law professors, and historians as one might wish for, and thus the importance of this collection. For decades, nay more than a century, the respectable members of the academy assured the public that such heresies as nullification and secession were long ago consigned to the dustbin of history, forever buried with the appropriate wooden stake through the heart via Lee's surrender at Appomattox. Not so, say our contributors, and not just in these United States. It seems that the forces and proponents of political consolidation throughout the globe are meeting with resistance, non-cooperation, material nullification, and even secession. The contributors to this volume are to be commended for attempting to understand these phenomena, both historic and contemporary, with detachment and fairness, and all the more since it is clear few if any of the contributors have much sympathy with nullification, secession, or its modern day proponents. Furthermore, the essays contain many fine insights into some of the more problematic aspects of the American political order.

As a point of fairness allow me to offer a fair disclosure on where I stand concerning the American political order. My specific training as a historian leaves me a bit suspicious of theory, though I confess an occasional foray into the field as a guilty pleasure. Contingency, and its role in change and continuity, seem to me the more significant movers in politics. For example, the Declaration of Independence becomes a mere curiosity in a failed provincial rebellion if the Maryland line makes the decision not to cover the retreat of Washington's forces at the battle of Long Island. The Philadelphia

Convention may have receded into memory in the same fashion had the independent states taken action against their representatives at the Convention for gravely exceeding their authority. Whether we like it or not, what happened at Philadelphia was a bold act of regime change, and not one representative, save those of New Jersey, at that gathering could legally claim the authority from their state to engage in such a revolutionary act. Thus, we are left with the fact that the United States was not born of one revolutionary act but two. This is, in my humble view, crucial.

Regime change by its nature invites experiment (did not many of the framers refer to the new federal republic as such?) and instability. True, many conservative voices at the Philadelphia Convention won important victories in erecting at least paper barriers to federal consolidation, or like John Dickinson, calling the members to trust more in the received wisdom and experience of self-government the former colonies enjoyed for many seasons, than the metaphysical nostrums of some of the more "egg-headed" at the convention. Nevertheless, it should be rather a sobering thought that a mere seventy two years after the ink dried on the parchment, the grandsons of the framers of the Constitution were shooting each other down in the country's bloodiest conflict to date. This may not be indicative of a failed state, but it is suggestive that there are important latent, and not so latent, sources of instability in the constitutional order of these United States.

So given my antifederalist tendencies and curmudgeonly outlook on these matters, I found it a pleasant surprise that many of the contributors to this volume recognized in the proponents of secession, interposition, and nullification sincere attempts to address the instabilities in the American political regime. Or to be clear, it is now in the pale of respectable scholarly discourse to view the unchecked centralization of power in the federal government as a threat to constitutional maintenance. Of course, one may argue that interposition, nullification, and secession also are credible threats to constitutional maintenance. Which raises the crucial question, "How is it that such diametrically opposed actions as the consolidation of power in the federal government, secession, nullification, and interposition can all be threats to the maintenance of the American constitutional order?"

Sanford Levinson provides a good starting place to tackle this question by asking a related question, "Is there a final authority at all? If so, who is it?" Ah, therein lay the rub. Those who might put forward the Supreme Court as that authority have some hurdles to clear. First, Article Three to the constitution never explicitly confers the power of judicial review upon the Supreme Court. Second, John Marshall, in the landmark case *Marbury v. Madison*, sneaks judicial review under the door. He never asserts the Supreme Court has this power, he just uses it. Third, Marshall may have used the power, but he never asserted in the decision that the Supreme Court had an exclusive authority to interpret the Constitution. Levinson also rightly criticizes what he calls the "Appomattox argument" and its proponents. This argument postulates that the Union victory in the War Between the States put to rest all debate concerning the legitimacy of secession and nullification. In my view, Levinson is correct for two reasons. Attempts at all sorts of practical nullification or interposition are bountiful in the post-war era: massive resistance in the South to forced public school integration, as well as more recent resistance to federal immigration law and narcotics laws at the state and local level. On a theoretical level, if one accepts that the consent of the governed is the foundation of political legitimacy, how is coercive military action directed at a politically conscious people, a people who define themselves as a separate political entity, a legitimate political act? One of the sillier answers to this question suggests that there was one definitive act of consent given by the "Founders" binding all progeny forever to the constitutional order of the Union. I have yet to find the document or contract detailing the particulars of this definitive act of consent, and I also recall that the Articles of Confederation were supposed to be "perpetual." It seems "revolution" is a part of the American political DNA, so that political regimes in America are perpetual until they are not. Thus Levinson's conclusion is apt, "one simply cannot understand American or world history without paying respectful attention to the reality of secession." Let the Church say amen!

No collection of this sort is complete without a consideration of James Madison and his views on interposition. To Jonathan Gienapp the task fell, and he gives us a valuable insight into the mind of a political Rube Goldberg (my view, not Gienapp's). As Gienapp points out, Madison was deeply concerned with how the American constitutional order might maintain itself through a crisis of overreach by a branch of the federal government or the entire federal government for that matter. Madison's remedy was to turn to "the people," who must be informed of the danger facing the republic and somehow activated to preserve the republic's constitutional order. Gienapp, who does admire Madison, honestly assesses Madison's remedy as insufficient. Madison is typically opaque on how the people are to be activated and what actions the people might undertake once they are activated. To be charitable, Madison probably knows that the road leads to some form of resistance against federal power, perhaps even revolution, and he did not wish to go there. Does this not prove the point that political regimes conceived in revolution may have particular difficulty with maintaining their constitutions?

James H. Read and Neal Allen contribute a piece that provides a historical overview of nullification and secession. Like Levinson's contribution, Read and Allen ask important and fundamental questions. The most valuable question they ask is whether the United States exists as a "deliberate political community?" In my view, Read and Allen correctly assert that the answer to this question is to be found more in the practice of American politics, and not in the "parchment." Here they echo, to a limited degree, John Randolph of Roanoke's criticism of the Constitution's "parchment barriers" and his advocacy of *praxis* by means of custom and tradition. While Read and Allen are not particularly favorable to "neo-nullification" advocates such as Tom Woods, yet Read's and Allen's emphasis on political *praxis,* as opposed to theory, suggests that Woods and his ilk may prove to be significant in terms of policy influence. If political trends continue to favor the resistance of the periphery (states and local communities) to the center (the federal government), then Woods and his ideas may exert real practical influence.

Other gems offered by the contributors include the following: Ernst Young's insight that concurrent jurisdiction has replaced dual federalism, and thus opened up new ways of resisting federal for states and local governments by refusing cooperation with federal enforcement efforts. Given the dependence of the federal government upon the cooperation of state and local governments to implement and enforce federal edicts and policies, non-cooperation is an effective and important means of peripheral resistance to the central government. In a similar vein, Mark A. Graber identifies ways in which "partial nullification" and interposition do function as effective means of resisting federal law. For example, the Supreme Court's view that jury verdicts cannot be impeached allows a good deal of room for jury nullification. Vicki Jackson also offers an important piece in her exploration of the global precedents of secession that exist. Ran Hirschl also strikes a blow against the view that secession and nullification are somehow American exceptions or aberrations. Indeed, he explores the uncomfortable truth for many globalists that "separatist impulses" are not going away, instead they may be gaining some momentum.

I must confess that I was a bit taken aback by the contribution of Jared Goldstein, whose main point seems to be that violent "private resistance" to perceived federal tyranny "flows naturally from the constitutional philosophy of the nullification movement." For Goldstein, nullification seems to lead "naturally" to violent insurrection, as it is merely one of the first tactics to be employed by those people who seek to resist a perceived federal injustice. There may well be people out there who do believe this, and rightly Goldstein does name the names of those he thinks fit the bill, but I rather doubt that if one holds to the doctrine of nullification in some form or other, one is then *ipso facto* an advocate or potential advocate of violent insurrection. I suggest that at least some advocates of nullification today and yesterday, especially its most able theorist John C. Calhoun, viewed nullification as a way to defuse potential violent conflicts. I might also suggest that any latent American tendencies toward violent insurrection, be it of the left or the right, may well have deeper roots than the emergence of nullification. The roots I refer to are, of course, the American Revolution and the violent insurrectionary acts which preceded it.

Unfortunately, space does not permit me to do justice to all of the contributors. It is an important work though, and one which deserves a close and fair reading. Certainly, not all of the perspectives of the contributors are shared by the members and supporters of the Abbeville Institute, and there are some perspectives here that many of us might reject outright. Nevertheless, the contributors have done a fine job of giving serious attention to important centrifugal trends in the American and transnational political order, trends which may continue to strengthen and gather momentum in the years ahead.

What We Have to Expect

A review of David Jonathan White, *How Radical Republican Antislavery Rhetoric and Violence Precipitated Secession, October 1859-April 1861*(Abbeville Institute Press, 2021)

One of the tragic casualties of America's long culture war is the distortion of the country's central event, The War Between the States. During the 1950s, historians such as Avery Craven began to question the "irrepressible conflict" thesis favored by most historians. As Bruce Catton wrote in a review of Craven's book, *The Coming of the Civil War*, Craven and "a highly industrious school of historians has been asking whether the war should have been fought at all and whether it was perhaps not more the fault of the North than of the South." Criticized at first for being revisionist, later assailed by the neo-abolitionist culture warriors of the 1960s as pro-Southern, Craven, and other historians seeking a detached and objective account of the war fell out of favor. In the last sixty years or so the historian as activist for the cause *du jour* now rules supreme in the departments of history in the United States. Causes and fashions may change, but one thing remains the same, an uncompromising assertion that slavery was the cause of the war and the accompanying demonization of the South.

Even in the hands of deft and balanced historians, the narrative of causation dominant in the field is simple and inflexible. Northern moral sensibilities became outraged over the existence of slavery in the United States as Southern anti-slavery voices went silent. As territorial expansion proceeded, the Northern moral impulse became steadfast in refusing to allow slavery to spread into the western territories, whereas Southerners insisted upon the spread of their peculiar institution into the same. With the election of a sectional president, Abraham Lincoln, committed to halting the westward expansion of slavery, even as he promised to not interfere with slavery where it existed, Southerners thought themselves and their institution threatened and decided to leave the Union. Thus, the war came. The more activist oriented and politically motivated historians add to the above interpretation condemnations of Southern racism, white supremacy, and a full embrace of the most wonderful and paranoid of American conspiracy theories, the evil machinations of the "Slave Power."

The careful reader and student of logic may have already identified several questions left unanswered by the dominant interpretation. First, if the South secedes, doesn't this effectively defuse the conflict regarding the spread of slavery to the territories? Second, why does the South feel threatened by Lincoln's election? True, the western territories would be closed, but the proposed Corwin Amendment supported by Mr. Lincoln would provide slavery with explicit and ironclad constitutional protection. Third, why exactly is the North adamant about opposing Southern secession? These unanswered questions invite a very thorough and patient study in several fields: history, semiotics, economics, and politics to achieve a satisfactory understanding as to why the war came, or more accurately, why secession and war—two quite different and distinct things—were chosen by the historical actors of the 1850s and 1860s.

Jonathan White does us the good service of attempting an answer to the second question, why is the South threatened by Mr. Lincoln's election? White frames the question in more narrow terms. What moved Southern moderates and Unionists who opposed secession in 1858 to embrace secession in 1860-61? White's answer to this question is more nuanced and complex than repeating the magic mantra "slavery." Some historical context is helpful in fully understanding White's argument. The Dred Scott decision in 1857 repealed the Missouri Compromise and opened the western territories to slaveholders and their property. Nevertheless, very few Southerners were taking their slaves into Kansas or any other territory. The "Slave Power" faltered badly at the very moment of its great triumph. Stephen Douglas, a senator from Illinois, was much more the hard-headed realist than the Slave Power conspiracy theorists. Douglas knew Southerners were reluctant to settle with their slaves in Kansas. Thus, his advocacy of the doctrine of "popular sovereignty," a political sleight of hand that obscured a *fait accompli*. In Douglas's correct view, antislavery settlers would quickly outnumber slaveholders in the territories and pass territorial and state constitutions outlawing slavery. Northerners need only be patient and the powers of the federal government would fall into their lap. Of course, Southerners could count too. They knew full well that the result of "popular sovereignty" would be a Congress and Presidency dominated by sectional interests resulting in a program of financial and political consolidation financed in large part by high tariffs. These issues were intertwined, much like a pile of fishhooks, where an attempt to remove one hook results in lifting the entire tangle of issues. Separating this tangle was no easy task.

Slavery was of course the political issue that generated the most excitement and division. The Dred Scott decision, the Fugitive Slave Act, and on the eve of war the proposed Corwin Amendment and its guarantee of federal protection of slavery in the states where it existed did not allay Southern fears regarding the abolition of slavery and its consequences. The Abolitionists and their intellectual progeny, who claimed the existence of a "Slave Power" bent on extending slavery throughout the Union, were immune to the lack of evidence of a vast Southern slaveholder migration extending throughout the country. The "Slave Power" conspiracy was useful to its adherents in explaining away judicial and legislative defeats, economic distress in the rural areas of the Old Northwest, the Panic of 1857, and the violence in Bleeding Kansas. The Republican triumph in the election of 1860 allayed Northern anxieties, but it elevated Southern fears. The Corwin Amendment was an olive branch designed to entice the already seceded states back into the Union, and to keep the wavering border states and upper South in the Union. Why did Southern politicians not jump at the Corwin Amendment, an amendment supported by the newly elected President Abraham Lincoln? What accounted for Southerner's deep distrust of Republicans and Northerners?

Jonathan White's important book addresses these questions. White begins where all good historians begin, by understanding historical actors as they understood themselves. Southern conservatives and Unionists are the focus of White's attention, they are the key swing vote whose views must change if secession is to become a reality in the South. Throughout much of the trying decade of the 1850s, these men of moderate and conservative principles remained steadfast in their attachment to the Union. By 1858, fear began to erode the attachment these men had to the Union and fear drove them to ultimately throw in with the secessionists. This fear was driven by the violent rhetoric and the violent actions of antislavery Northerners and the inability of many conservative Northerners to oppose and universally condemn the same.

The divisive and polarizing rhetoric of Northern antislavery politicians first emerged in force during the debates over the admission of Missouri as a "slave state." By the late 1850s, however, the rhetoric of many antislavery politicians and intelligentsia grew violent in its imagery and its proposals, and it was not limited to just a few select partisan politicians and newspaper editors. Throughout the North, politicians and the intelligentsia lent their active material support to those, like John Brown, seeking to incite a violent slave insurrection. John Brown's raid stoked the fires of division, but the rhetoric of Lysander Spoon, Brown's canonization by Ralph Waldo Emerson, the financial and material support given to Brown by the not so "Secret Six," and the failure of Northerners as a body to condemn antislavery violence. In some cases, some of Brown's people were shielded from extradition to Virginia. These factors drove many Southern conservatives and Unionists into the secessionist camp. Without this shift, secession was at best a doubtful prospect. As White demonstrates, the Brown raid became the lens through which the South viewed any suspicious actions, persons, or crimes. Quickly thereafter, the South took steps to secure its internal security.

As the election of 1860 neared, Southern fears for their internal security were not allayed. Democratic candidate for president, Stephen Douglas, adamantly opposed secession as a remedy for Southern security fears. To his credit, Abraham Lincoln condemned the actions of John Brown, but Southerners wanted much more from the man who authored the "House Divided" speech. As for the other leading Republican candidate, William Seward, the best he could muster on the antislavery violence issue was silence. It is no small wonder that the electoral victory of the Republicans, which for the first time placed the reigns of the federal government in the hands of a sectional party, was read by many Southerners, radical and moderate, as a sign of the North's bad intentions. The lower South seceded. The upper South hesitated, until Lincoln's unconstitutional call for militia and his military occupation of Maryland left no doubts in their minds. The trend was confirmed, the North had chosen the path of political violence to resolve the crisis.

White's book is important not because it provides us with a fuller understanding of why Southerners chose secession. His evidence is broad, encompassing the written and spoken word, as well as empirical data on the vote shifts in the secession conventions from union to separation, and the internal security preparations undertaken by Southern counties and states. White also offers a balanced account, he affirms that Southerners at times overreacted to rumors of abolitionist interference with slavery in local areas or to crimes of uncertain origin, but their response was understandable given the rise of the culture of political violence. The result is a provocative work. White examines how the threat of Northern political violence, what some may refer to as terrorism, impelled many Southerners of conservative and Unionist sentiment to view secession as the most prudent and reasonable course of action given the circumstances. Indirectly, White's book introduces the vital role violence and the threat of violence played in both the antislavery movement's actions and rhetoric and in the political culture of the North. Certainly, the advocacy of and material support given to violence on the part of large numbers of prominent and influential Northerners was an essential cause for many Southerners to embrace secession. Jonathan White not only broadens and deepens our understanding of the causes of secession, but he reveals the significant role public violence played in the political culture of the North, a topic that needs further and deeper study.

It is a paradox, but the time is both inopportune and opportune for such a study as Mr. White's. It is inopportune in that the academy is in no mood for a consideration of the dark side of the antislavery cause. The 1850s was prelude to the brutal and savage actions of the Federal war machine in Georgia, South Carolina, and Virginia—all in the service of a "righteous cause." Moral crusades attended by public violence is an old game with a deep tradition up North, especially in New England. Examination of conscience is not a strong suit of the Yankee intelligentsia. In these days of woke rage in which we find ourselves, Mr. White's book will be dismissed as Confederate apologia at best. Yet for those with eyes to see, Mr. White sets a rhyme of history before us. Call it what you will: critical race theory, cancel culture, the reign of "wokedom," or cultural Marxism, the self-righteous indignation is the same, the hypocrisy has not changed, the calls for violence echo the past. Mr. White's Southern Unionists did not see the danger until it was upon them, but they acted in a way that they viewed as necessary to their security and preservation. In the past the lines of conflict fell along well defined geographic and political boundaries. The boundaries are less well defined today, at best they resemble the old court and country conflicts of the colonial period. Yet one cannot come away from Mr. White's book without a sense of here we are again.

Regardless of the times, Mr. White has taken a large step in moving the discourse on the war and secession away from the simplistic cant and mantra of "slavery." He has deepened our understanding of why Southerners embraced secession and opened new paths for historical inquiry. One can ask for little more from a scholar toiling in the field of history. My one quibble is the title. The original title, *What We Have to Expect: Antislavery Violence and Secession, October 1859-1861* captures better the mindset of Southern Unionists who embraced secession. It also makes sense to substitute "Abolitionist" for "Antislavery" as the latter contained many diverse and more peaceful views on how to address the issue of slavery, the abolitionists embraced violence, some in deed, nearly all in word. Nevertheless, future generations of scholars who come after our post-rational era will be grateful to White for illuminating a crucial aspect of secession.

Rhetoric, Reality, and
the Late Unpleasantness

The 1850s is viewed by most scholars as the crucial decade of the sectional crisis that resulted in the War Between the States. The Great Triumvirate of John C. Calhoun, Henry Clay, and Daniel Webster had passed from the scene. These giants were replaced by lesser lights, and "the war came" as Mr. Lincoln claimed. As historical explanations go, there are worse. One may already discern the protests of the "righteous cause" crowd crying out against my neglect of the slavery issue, which we are told *ad infinitum, ad nauseum* was the sole cause of the great conflict. If only this were true.

The reality of the matter is a great deal more complex. As Avery Craven, Michael Holt, and most recently David Goldfield have argued, there was a great American political failure in the 1850s, due in part to the rise of a mediocre and radicalized set of politicians across the union, The sainted Mr. Lincoln himself was unable to find a way out of the morass of conflict. The table was set for war much earlier than the 1850s. The great Missouri Conflict and Compromise, whose fiftieth anniversary will soon be upon us, was the great catalyst for war. Northern sincerity regarding their opposition to slavery is debatable, what is not up for debate is that the rhetoric and the results of the compromise left the union geographically divided. Calhoun, Clay, and Webster were able to forestall the coming conflict for four decades, but the poison of that great political contest remained, lay dormant, but always threatening to awaken once more. This poison was the American penchant for mistaking the symbolic for the real, and in doing so jettisoning the native pragmatism upon which the union was constructed. Here lay the "ying and yang" of the American political character: on the one hand Americans displayed a remarkable ability to ground themselves in political realities and forge necessary compromises, yet many Americans were also susceptible to the seduction of powerful symbols and images conveying the idea that the American was an exceptional and even elect human being. It is this latter "yang" that is at the root of most of the mischief in American politics. The case of the Missouri conflict is powerful evidence of this.

The facts of the Missouri conflict are, or were, known by every schoolboy and girl in America. Missouri sought admission into the Union as a state where property in slaves was recognized by the Missouri constitution. Representatives and Senators, primarily from New York, but with significant support from their colleagues in New England and parts of the Old Northwest, resisted Missouri's entrance into the Union unless the state made provisions to exclude protections for slave property from its constitution. After much haggling, the Missouri Compromise was hammered out. Missouri would enter the union as a "slave state," Maine would be allowed to secede from Massachusetts and enter the union as a "free state," and a line was drawn at the southern border of Missouri, 36° 30′, across the old Louisiana Purchase. Territory below this line was to be open to slavery, north of the line save Missouri was closed to slavery. Historians of an earlier generation pointed the finger at New York for causing the trouble out of its resentment for Virginia's dominance of the executive branch, and its general prominence in the national councils. The "righteous cause" types who came along later praised the emerging egalitarian sensibilities of Northern congressmen as they awakened to the great evil of slavery and hoped to place limits upon its westward march. The earlier generation of scholars are closer to the mark, but what is missing from all analyses of the debate was the role the rhetoric of antislavery Northern politicians played in creating a sectional conflict that proved immune to any compromise or peaceful remedy. It was a case of political well-poisoning *par excellence.*

What were the major objections to protecting the holding of slave labor in Missouri? Northern politicians structured their argument around a secular Puritan dualistic worldview of opposing principles. In this simplistic and fatalistic view either slavery or freedom would triumph and stamp its mark upon the union. True to their Puritan intellectual masters, the antislavery congressmen relied upon *pathos,* the *argumentum in terrorem*, and the jeremiad in their rhetoric. Thus, the white freedmen of the North were the elect, slavery the original sin, and the South was the wilderness that threatened to overwhelm the city on the hill. The covenant, that is the American union, was imperiled by the moral, racial, and political dangers inherent in slavery. If slavery was not restricted to the "wilderness" of the South, America's divinely ordained mission to be a light unto the nations would be terminated. This rhetorical stance adopted by Northern congressmen would sow the seeds of permanent division among Americans, not reconciliation.

One need not take my word for this; the *Annals of Congress* for the Sixteenth Congress bear witness to all of this. There one may read Senator Rufus King's speech that slavery sapped American power, degraded free labor, and foreshadowing Lincoln's House Divided speech declared, "Freedom and slavery are the parties which stand this day before the Senate; and upon its decision the empire of one or the other will be established." Representatives John Taylor of New York and William Plumer, Jr. of New Hampshire echoed King's fear that slave labor degraded free labor and was of inferior value to free labor. Plumer viewed both slaves and slaveholders as both the serpent and the curse who "placed in a land flowing with milk and honey, would convert even the garden of Eden into a desert and a waste." Many Northern Congressmen took the opportunity the debates presented to draw important distinctions between North and South. In speech after speech the South was presented as a barren wasteland filled with slovenly whites, haughty and arrogant slaveholders addicted to idleness and luxury, and dangerous Africans. Representative Waller Taylor of Pennsylvania described his home state as a garden, filled with a hard-working "neat, blooming, animated, rosy-cheeked, peasantry;" Maryland, however, was a "barren waste" tilled by "hordes of slaves" whose distinguishing features were their "slow-motion" and "squalidness." The Northern press often echoed similar sentiments. The *New Hampshire Patriot* was typical. It lauded the "well cultivated, though rough fields of New England" flourishing under the hands of a "diligent and laborious" free, white population. The South, meanwhile, was the wasteland of miserable and idle whites. Taylor of New York and others viewed slavery as the "original sin" of the South. Taylor warned the House that if it failed to restrict slavery from Missouri, they would be guilty of the sin of the Pharisees, "when we deplore its [slavery's] existence—shall we not expose ourselves to the same kind of exposure which was pronounced by the Savior of Mankind, who builded the tombs of the prophets and garnished the sepulchers of the righteous and said, if they have lived in the days of their fathers they would not have been partakers with them in the blood of the prophets... ." The message was clear. Restrict slavery from Missouri or face the end of the American dream, the "Southernization" of the union, the presence of African Americans in the North, and the vengeance of God. And this just a small representation of what is available in the speeches of Northerners and the editorials of the Northern press.

The Northern argument drew upon good old fashioned secular Puritan dualism and scare tactics, but it also contained one innovation. Several Northern congressmen argued that the equality clause in the Declaration of Independence justified their position on Missouri's admission. Taylor of New York and Roberts of Pennsylvania went so far as to describe the Declaration as "the great cornerstone of all our laws and constitutions," in effect the American covenant. During the debate, the argument was unconvincing. In part, given Northern restrictions upon the freedom of free African-Americans, invoking the equality clause was a bit rich. The elevation of the Declaration to covenant status also suffered from being inaccurate. A junior representative from Kentucky, one Richard Mentor "I killed Tecumseh" Johnson, gave the proper and accepted definition of the Declaration's equality clause, "The meaning of this sentence is defined in its application; that all communities stand upon an equality; that Americans are equal with Englishman and have the right to organize such government for themselves as they shall choose...." No one on the other side answered Johnson and so the great error was laid to rest, but only for a time.

Southern congressmen were taken aback by all of this. The portrayal of the South, and Southerners white and black, was at best a caricature. Mostly, it was untrue, but given the American weakness of mistaking the symbolic for the real, a weakness particularly found in the children of the Puritan diaspora, true or false made little difference. Southern congressmen, still resistant at the time to Puritan fantasies, tended to argue the law and history against their opponents in the Missouri debate, and were correct about the legality and the historical precedents supporting their position to admit Missouri as a "slave state." But it was naïve a tactic. Those opposing Missouri's admission into the Union were not interested in historical or legal precedents. They were interested in a vision of American power and greatness that demonized and excluded both white and black Southerners. More importantly Northerners won a great victory. A line at was 36° 30′ drawn across the continent. A geographic line was now drawn upon maps and in the imaginations of men and women that demarcated the line between the fruitful, city on the hill of the North, and the benighted and barren wilderness of the South. It was a crucial rhetorical victory, for Northerners could ever after point to the lines, Mason Dixon and 36° 30′ as real and imaginary boundaries between the elect and the benighted. The rhetoric used to make such a line possible excluded any hopes for peaceful reconciliation by 1860 and has exercised a powerful influence upon the minds of Americans to this very day, acting as a lens of distortion through which we have viewed the history of our country.

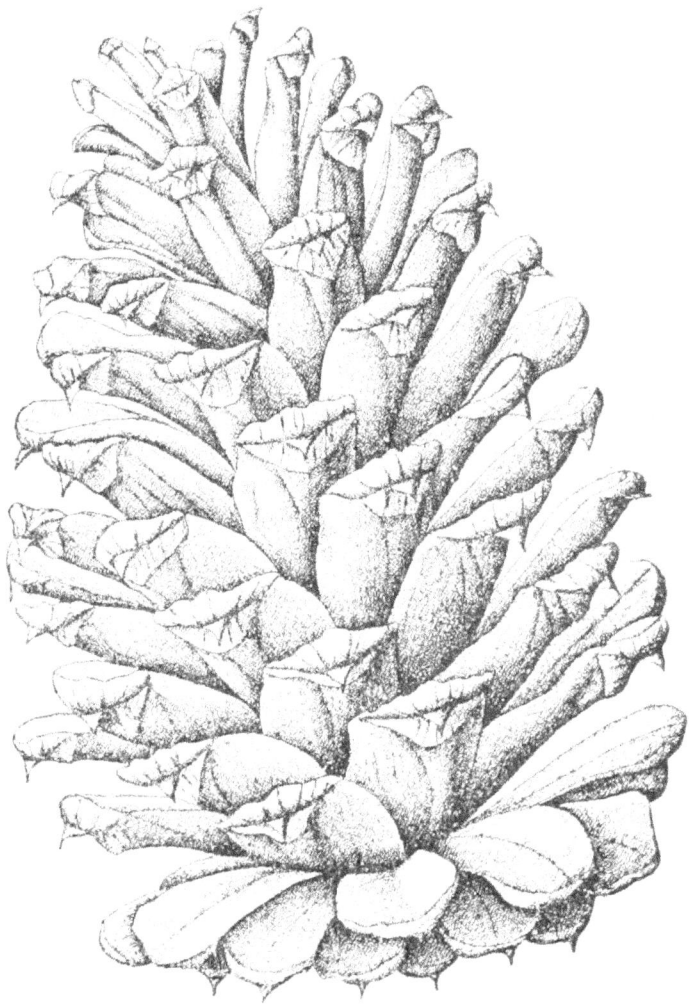

Southern Populism and
the South's Agrarian Identity

In what passes for political and cultural discourse today, the term "populist" is something of a pejorative, conjuring up images in the mind of the cultural and academic elite of dangerous folks with pitchforks and guns riding about in pick-up trucks looking for an uprising to foment. This of course is nonsense. What the tsars of public opinion describe as populism bears little resemblance to the real thing. The historian Richard Hofstatdter started the whole business of populist as dangerous rube, though he did concede the populists had some good ideas. Of course, Hofstadter also believed that the more polished and respectable and less hayseed progressives were needed to move the whole business of reform forward to an orderly and respectable conclusion. Contemporary historians tend to emphasize the constituent elements of the larger populist movement; one can find fine work done on the independent black populist movement or the precursors to the populists. The populist failure as a third party, the populist failure to forge an alliance with industrial labor, the populist failure to alleviate racial tensions and animosities in the South, and the failure of the populists to act as a catalyst for the creation of a European style labor party has captured the interest of left-leaning historians, as one might expect.

The historian who in my view comes closest to understanding the populist moment in the broader context of American history is Frederick Jackson Turner. Turner observed in *The Frontier in American History*, "Taken as a whole, Populism is a manifestation of the old pioneer ideals ... with the added element of increasing readiness to utilize the national government to effect ends." Turner understood three things: populism was American and not European, populism was agrarian, and that populists submitted to the political realities following the surrender at Appomattox and would seek not to leave the Union, but to take control of the federal government. Other historians have plowed the fields of late nineteenth century and early twentieth century American culture, politics, and economics, and the place of the populists within this context. I wish to re-examine the populists in a broader historical context and according to the model of court versus country which emerged as powerful driver in the sixteenth century conflicts in Britain and in British North America and remain a good explanatory model for many of the divisions and conflicts that emerge in American history and in contemporary America as well.

The origins of populism go back to a certain suspicion among the colonial and later settlers of America's frontiers that the folks back in the political and urban centers of America were out of touch with the realities of, shall we say, country living. Bacon's Rebellion in Virginia, 1676, offers a fascinating study of this phenomena. To this day, historians dispute the triggers that set the whole rebellion in motion, but we do know that folks in the farther districts were quite upset with both the Indian policy and the land policy of Governor Berkely, and they were not above marching on Jamestown to express their intense dissatisfaction regarding these matters. People of all races and classes were involved in the uprising. This had the effect of terrifying what then passed for city folk in Virginia. Virginia's later passage of a more stringent slave code was viewed by Edmund Morgan as a means to deflect country folk resentment away from the political elite and toward black folks, but it may also have been passed in response to the explosion in the number of African slaves being transported to Virginia. The regulator movements in the Carolinas also exhibited a court versus country dynamic in that country people were once again dissatisfied with the "court's" handling of land policy, the administration of justice, and public finance.

In the eighteenth century, Country Whigs and Country Tories developed a critique of the emerging union between consolidated finance and central government as it took form under Prime Minister Robert Walpole. In its broad outlines, the argument of the Country Party decried the cozy relationship between financiers, merchants, and the Parliament, and the ability of Walpole and his ministers to manipulate the Parliament through the granting of charters, monopolies, offices, and subsidies. Lord Bolingbroke, the leading Country Tory of the day, argued for the country gentry and nobility to ascend to leadership positions in Great Britain to preserve the country's virtue. Since these folks enjoyed a certain self-sufficiency and independence derived from their estates, and were removed from other corrupting urban influences, Bolingbroke believed the landed class would better resist the temptations proffered by Walpole and his associates and rid the country of both its corruption and the government's dangerous flirtation with men of capital.

Social and economic conditions in Great Britain during Bolingbroke's time undermined the appeal to public virtue he made to the landed classes. Many of the nobility and wealthier gentry had considerable economic interests tied up in Great Britain's mercantile and financial endeavors. If the appeal to the landed folks fell flat in Great Britain, it won adherents in British Colonial America, especially among the planters of the Tidewater. The Country Party worldview provided the leadership of the Southern colonies with a powerful tool to interpret the intentions behind British fiscal and taxation policies in the 1760s. The British levying of duties and internal taxes upon the colonies, combined with the collapse of the tobacco price and the drying up of credit, caused many planters to write about the attempts of the "corrupt" British Parliament and the attempts of the British to "enslave" the colonists. This was not hyperbole; the tidewater planters meant every word. Moreover, they saw in themselves the virtuous landholders Bolingbroke and other Country Party writers praised as the source of virtue in the state. Those areas of the Southern countryside that supported the American Revolution, opposed the ratification of the Constitution, and supported Thomas Jefferson's Republican Party echoed the themes in their protest British rule first articulated by the Country Party's adherents.

The court versus country dynamic was crystalized and institutionalized in the conflict between Alexander Hamilton and Thomas Jefferson. The fundamental issue separating Hamilton and Jefferson was the former's conviction that an alliance between capital and government was necessary for the stability and sustainability of the federal government, and Jefferson's view that such an alliance would lead to a consolidation of both capital and political power that would both threaten the liberties of the states and the citizenry and increase corruption in the body politic. The first round of the fight between these two outlasted their lives and ended in victory for the Jeffersonian Camp. By 1848, Hamilton's national bank scheme was dead, replaced by the Independent Treasury, protective tariff rates were beginning to slowly trend down, federally funded internal improvements were ruled unconstitutional, and the territorial expansion of the United States seemed to secure the agrarian interest well into the future. Opponents of the agricultural interest deftly linked the issues of territorial expansion and the issue of slavery to sow the seeds of sectional division. It mattered little that the expansion of slavery into the territories was more of a legal abstraction than a concrete reality, it blew the Whig Party apart and fed the rise of the Republican Party. The Republican Party, the country's first and most successful sectional party, became the new standard bearers for the old Hamilton and Whig programs. The Republicans commanded a majority in the House of Representatives and the presidency by 1860 and were positioned to control the Senate within a year or two. Given the rancor over the slavery question, and the political realities facing Southerners, it would have been surprising if Southern states did not attempt to secede.

Even if one believes the fairy tale that slavery was the sole, only, and everlasting cause of the War Between the States, it does not negate the fact that the Southern states who seceded, and those forgotten border states who tried to secede, were agrarian societies assaulted by a Republican "court" bent on imposing the Hamiltonian type program of national consolidation. It was a classic case of center versus periphery, the great continuity of American political history. The South's defeat in the war placed its agrarian society in an extremely vulnerable situation. The combination of disenfranchisement, the introduction of share-cropping and tenant farming, the destruction of people, land and capital, and the massive increases in property taxes on an already destitute population were devastating in their economic and social effects. Most Southerners rejected a "long war" option against the federal nemesis and its military occupation of the region in favor of "Redemption." But Redemption was only made possible by the razor thin election of 1876, and the willingness of Republicans to bring an end to Reconstruction to secure the White House.

The peace effected by the Compromise of 1877 did not last long. Weather conditions, politics, and economics converged to bestir the country districts, both South and West, into considerable restlessness and deep discontent. In the West, unusually wet conditions prevailed in the 1880s just as the Dakotas, Nebraska, and Kansas were settled, giving farmers a false sense of how well watered the region was. In 1887, persistent drought began to rule the weather. Drought, coupled with falling grain prices due to international competition began to tighten credit in the farm districts, and served as a rude reminder how dependent farmers were upon both the grace of God and the almighty loan. The woes of the agrarian districts of the South we have already cataloged; Southern farmers were also exposed to international competition in cotton production, and more than ever the farmers of the South's upcountry districts found themselves ever more closely tied into the nexus of credit, finance, and international competition. This exposure to the credit markets and international competition explained the continued expansion of cotton production in the South. Also cotton, unlike most other agricultural commodities, could be held off the market, and it was liquid, farmers often referred to their harvested cotton as "money in the bank." Given the economic thralldom in which the South was held, the regime of high tariffs, discriminatory freight rates, and tight credit, the money often was found in the banks of Northern financial institutions.

When the populist eruption broke onto the scene of American politics, it was primarily a movement of Southern agrarians. All the leadership of the movement and the Populist Party were farmers or had significant ties to the land. The foremost example of the latter was Tom Watson, a lawyer, a newspaper editor, and a farmer. The widespread expansion of the telegraph and railroad brought the South's rural districts direct daily exposure to the new industrial world, just as the local bankers, supply merchants, and country stores integrated the rural South into the credit nexus of late nineteenth century America. This exposure to modern industrial America was subtle; daily life still followed many of the patterns established in the antebellum period. Rural churches, many still served by itinerant preachers, were the central focus of community life, and not just the spiritual life of rural communities. Often, they served as local meeting places where affairs temporal were addressed, the forerunner of the Populist Party, the Farmers' Alliance, held local chapter meetings in these churches. The courthouse and the local country store also served as an important center of community life.

Even as the new industrial world made its presence felt in the rural South, the communities therein were still homogenous in culture and conducted their relations on a personal, face-to face basis.

Rapidly, exposure turned into intrusion as the world of the rural South found the conditions of its daily life being increasingly influenced, and in some aspects determined by people and conditions far removed from their communities. The proponents of the industrialized New South began to reach their country cousins via city dailies and county weeklies. The pressing need for marketing facilities for crops and credit brought the people of the rural South into confrontation with more impersonal interactions with larger organizations who provided, or did not provide, these services. Monetary and price deflation, in part a result of policies engineered in faraway New York and Washington D. C., squeezed many Southern and Western farmers out of profitability. The Coinage Act of 1873, which ended bi-metallism and the production of silver dollars by the United States Treasury, combined with increased industrial and agricultural production resulted in widespread deflation. Crop prices, however, fell faster than the manufactured goods farmers relied upon to stay in business. As farms in the South and West underwent a slow but sure mechanization trend, the effects of crop price deflation on many farmers' profit margins made the purchase of innovative capital goods like the Deere plow, grain drills, new mechanized reapers, and binders, and the first steam tractors an impossibility.

Not every farmer in the South and West went under, many weathered the challenges of the late nineteenth century and a few even prospered. What did reign supreme in the rural areas of the South was prevalent insecurity. People witnessed their indebted neighbors, folks with whom they attended church, to whom they may have been related by blood or marriage, whose lives they shared daily go under. Many of these people who lost their farms were good farmers, this reality undermined the old assurance that farming brought security and self-sufficiency.

The country response to what was viewed as the predations of the "court" was to bind together in organizations and oppose the far away metropolitans who rural people believed exercised an inordinate and malicious influence upon their lives. Cooperative organizations, such as The Patrons of Husbandry and others, began to spring up throughout the rural South and West. The cooperative movement attempted to pool resources to purchase the latest technology for common use, share best agricultural practices, and assist distressed neighbors. The creation of the Farmers' Alliance in 1875 followed a similar cooperative pattern Ranchers in Lampas, Texas acted in cooperation to round up strays, hang horse thieves, and seek other avenues for mutually beneficent action. Under Charles Macune, the son of a Methodist minister, the Farmers' Alliance developed into a political and cooperative organization, and by the 1880s they actively sought alliances with the farmers' alliance organizations in the North and the Knights of Labor. At the same time Black farmers founded the Colored Farmers' Alliance and Cooperative Union, which was especially influential for a time in Texas and North Carolina. In the 1880s, Farmers' Alliance candidates were successfully contesting state elections in the South and West.

By 1892 the Populist Party burst onto the national scene and became the main torchbearer of the country's resistance to the court. The ideas that animated the party and informed the actions and policies of the Populist Party came from several sources. From the Jeffersonian tradition the Populists received their view of farming and labor as wealth producing activities, while holding finance and credit in suspicion for not producing tangible wealth. Like Thomas Jefferson, the Populists viewed farming as an important locus of virtue. The Jacksonian tradition reinforced the Populists' fear of national banks and financiers, and their willingness to use political means on the federal level to limit the influence of these institutions and people. The Populist Party's Omaha Platform made wise of language that harkened back to concepts that traced back to Country Party. Repeatedly the Platform expressed concerns with the injustice, the corruption of morals, the need for virtue, the fear of financial and economic enslavement, the country as the locus of public virtue, all concepts that the Country Party, the Southern patriots of the American Revolution, Jefferson and Jackson's people, John C. Calhoun and his people, and many Confederates supported. In addition, strong religious overtones from the evangelical tradition exerted their influence, as one minister declared that Populism stood for the "morals of Christ and politics of Thomas Jefferson."

The policies of the Populist Party reflected many of the old country concepts as they were expressed through time, but Populists also embraced the notion of wresting control of the federal government from the court and using its powers to benefit the country. Some Populist policies echoed those of the old Jeffersonians and Jacksonians, the independent federal sub-treasury system. A unique feature of the Populist version of the subtreasury was that farmers would be given storage facilities for their crops at the sub treasuries and could borrow up to 80% of the value of their store crop from the sub treasury. The Populist support for ending protective tariffs was also centered in the Jeffersonian and Southern political tradition. Populist monetary policy was a mixed bag, most favored a re-monetization of silver, and a few favored a fiat paper currency. In other policy areas the Populists launched a campaign of direct action by the federal government on consolidated capital. They supported a graduated income tax, government ownership of railroads, telegraph and telephone, and the direct election of senators. Populists believed this last reform would combat the influence of railroad executives over the selection of senators by state legislatures. The Populists also believed, and not without reason, that many state legislative assemblies were controlled or heavily influenced by the railroad companies. Additional democratic reforms favored by the Populist Party included the recall of lawmakers, and the right of the people to influence legislation or directly legislate via petition and referendum.

Many of the policies of the Populists favored the very government consolidation seen as dangerous to public virtue and opposed by the heirs to the principles of the Country Party. Indeed, how could the Populists who looked to the Jeffersonian tradition for inspiration advocate for such policies? This is a fair question. The Jacksonian heritage the Populists also drew from was more open to aggressive federal action than the Jeffersonians. The settlement of Appomattox, as well as the influence of the railroads in the state legislatures, made appeals to state sovereignty moot in the view of many Populists. At work too was a certain amount of political naivete on the part of many Populists. Both the Democrats and Republicans had powerful incentives to undermine the Populists by all means fair and foul, and Populists overestimated their ability to capture the federal government and to overcome the significant divisions within their own ranks. Nor did the Populists foresee the problem of regulatory capture that has married large capital to large government in perpetual union. It was the combination of internal divisions, effective political campaigning by the Democrats and Republicans, and co-option of many of the policies of the Populists by progressives in both the Democrat and Republican parties that led to the Populist Party's demise.

The Populist legacy is often measured by the policies of the party that were incorporated into the political life of America. There were successes here: the graduated income tax, petition, recall, referendum, and direct election of senators. None have had the specific effect hoped for by the Populists, namely limiting the influence of wealth and consolidated capital in the councils of the nation and holding politicians directly accountable to the people. The true legacy of the Populist party was that it was the last great agrarian revolt, the last mass resistance offered by the country against an urbanized court of political and financial consolidationists. As such it does still loom large in the minds of our political and financial elite. Populist remains a pejorative term and continues to operate as an expression of the fear the elite have of rural folk and the common person when they do not mind their political place. Given the economic, cultural, and political destitution of the rural South, and rural America in general, such an irrational fear on the part of the elite class is evidence the old conflict between court and country still plays a formative role in the political imagination of America.

WHERE THE GRAPES OF WRATH ARE STORED:
THE RECONSTRUCTION OF SOUTHERN RELIGION

Fundamentalism is often viewed as the most Southern of religions. Yet this is not so. It was an alien seed planted in ground razed by war and harrowed by Reconstruction. The harrowing, or Reconstruction if one prefers, was not merely an updating of the constitutional and political order in the South, but an attempt to impose a new social, cultural, and religious order upon the ruins of the old. To best understand this process, the temptation to isolate the reconstruction of Southern religion must be avoided. There is an important, wider historical context concerning the religious life of modern man to be kept in mind, a context that affected Catholic and Protestant belief and worship.

As the late Middle Ages transitioned to the early modern era in European history, a subtle shift in western Christianity emerged. Religious life in Europe, once characterized primarily by communal worship and devotion began to shift toward individualized devotion and spirituality. An example of this shift occurred in Northern Europe and was known as the *Devotio Moderna*. This new form of devotion emphasized personal piety, scripture study in the original languages, moral reform, simplicity in devotions, penance, and the pursuit of personal sanctity. A group of lay and clerical associations, the best known being the Sisterhood and Brotherhood of the Common Life, were devoted to this new, modern devotion. The Brotherhood of the Common Life also dedicated themselves to the education of both lay men and clerics, such luminaries of the Northern Renaissance as Saint Thomas More and Erasmus received part or all their education from the Brotherhood of the Common Life. The most singular work of the modern devotion Thomas a Kempis's, *The Imitation of Christ*, emphasized the Christian's personal relationship with Jesus Christ, and was found in the libraries of both Catholics and Protestants. Protestant emphasis upon the individual's relationship with the person of Jesus Christ is well documented, but this same emphasis was also present in the Catholic Reformation before and after the Council of Trent. Saint Ignatius's spiritual exercises and Carmelite meditation are two outstanding examples.

The modern devotion's emphasis upon the individual's spiritual life began to fuse with a late medieval philosophical movement, nominalism, resulting in the elevation of emotion as a guide to one's religious life and spiritual state. In general, nominalists were skeptical regarding the powers of reason to ascertain and understand being or essence. This included Being itself, namely God. By limiting the intellectual faculty's role in the discernment of the true, the good, and the beautiful, nominalists, either explicitly or by default, came to rely on revelation as the only sure guide in spiritual matters, particularly scripture. For the individual believer, revelation and emotion would gradually take more of the ground once occupied by the intellectual faculty in the spiritual life. In the world of evangelical Christianity, emotion played a singular role in the conversion experience of many Christians.

The turmoil created by religious conflicts, the new commercial order, and the rise of the nation-state in the sixteenth and seventeenth centuries had an enormous effect upon the religious life of British North America. Secular rulers throughout Europe, both Catholic and Protestant, began to assert their authority over the churches within their realms. The Peace of Augsburg enshrined this new order within the confines of the Holy Roman Empire, as the head of state decide upon the religious confession of his subjects. Both Martin Luther and Henry VIII asserted the right of a prince to be the head of the Church within his realm, the views of the Gallicans expressed similar sentiments with respect to the powers of the French monarch over the Church within the borders of France. In the British Isles, control of the state became a matter of paramount concern for Catholics, Anglicans, and Puritans throughout the 1600s. Indeed, the religious question would remain unsettled in the British Isles until the Glorious Revolution.

The religious conflicts between Anglicans, Catholics, Puritans, and other dissenters are well known. An example of the complexity of these conflicts can be found in an examination of the Battle of Worcester in 1651. An odd bed fellows alliance of mostly Scottish and English Presbyterians, Anglicans, and a sprinkling of Catholics, fought against Cromwell's Puritans for the establishment of the future Charles II upon the throne of his ill-fated father, Charles I. George Mason's ancestor, "the Cavalier," fought in the royalist side in this uprising, and fled to Virginia after the royalist defeat. Mason's family, which was at least nominally Anglican, was rumored to contain a crypto Catholic or two, not an entirely uncommon thing in the west of England in the mid seventeenth century. All of this suggests that the political and religious situation in the British Isles was topsy turvy.

The "Anglican Solution" achieved via the Glorious Revolution was limited in its success. The terms of the solution were simple, the Anglican Church was the established Church, the monarch of England was its head, believe what you wish, but do show up for weekly services, do pay your tithe, and do not antagonize your neighbor. Penal laws were imposed upon Catholics, and to a lesser degree Protestant dissenters, to ensure compliance. The system did not transfer well to the settlements in British North America. Established churches, Anglican and Puritan, found themselves under the heel of colonial governments in short order. To be an "established church" meant that one received state support, financial and otherwise, from the colonial government, but toleration of dissenters was a matter of state policy with little input from the church. It was common for colonial governments in the eighteenth century to license preachers from dissenting groups or allow for the building of places of worship by non-Trinitarian believers such as the Society of Friends, who also had their own colony in Pennsylvania. Even penal laws restricting the public activities of Catholics were sometimes strictly enforced and at other times lax in enforcement in those colonies where such laws were on the books. Finally, there was simply too much space for a colonial government to effectively manage the religious affairs of a colony much beyond the coastal settlements. These conditions facilitated the religious pluralism of British North America.

The religious pluralism of the antebellum South was characterized by geography and modes of worship and belief. At the periphery of the South's northern and southern ends were the Catholics of Maryland and Louisiana. Along much of the eastern coast of the South, Episcopalians held sway, along with a smattering of Lutherans, Baptists, Presbyterians, Catholics, and Jews. Further inland one might run into the Quaker and Moravian settlements of North Carolina. The true heart of Southern religion, however, was to be found in the Methodists and Baptists who embraced the evangelical style. Puritanism, and its attendant concepts of the Elect, the wilderness, and the city on the hill did not gain significant traction in the South until after the War Between the States. What Puritanism in the South that existed at this time was confined primarily to Presbyterians, one voice among many in the diverse tapestry of Southern religion, and many of these Calvinists of the backcountry South placed a much higher value upon liberty than the teleological commitments of the Northeastern Puritan. In the First Great Awakening, Presbyterians viewed the under educated and uneducated Baptist and Methodist circuit preachers with suspicion; the feeling was often mutual.

In the antebellum South, because of the First Great Awakening, the Evangelical mode of belief and worship dominated the South. The Evangelical mode emphasized a direct and personal relationship with Jesus Christ, established by the Holy Spirit, producing an emotional conversion experience. The conversion experience, or "New Birth," was marked by a new life of holiness, religious devotion, moral discipline, and missionary zeal. Preachers of this fresh style made emotional appeals attacking sin and sinfulness and offering salvation via conversion. Appeals to the potential convert's reason were rejected; for the Evangelical conviction and conversion was centered in the heart, not the mind.

The Evangelical style bound together both black and white, free and slave in one religious cultural expression. Many churches in the antebellum South were integrated, with separate seating for the races. The integration of congregations was especially prevalent among the Methodists and Baptists, a situation that did not change until after the War Between the States. Catholic and Methodist congregations in Louisiana remained integrated almost until the end of the nineteenth century.

The antebellum South was by no means a religious Nirvana, but there was a large degree of tolerance and respect among people of different faiths. As to be expected in a Protestant country, the greatest antagonism existed between Catholics and Protestants. This antagonism was evidenced by the repeal of Act of Toleration in Maryland in the seventeenth century, legal restrictions and proscriptions placed on Catholics in the Southern colonies and later states, and often sharp theological debates between the clergy in the newspapers of the day.

Notwithstanding these tensions, Catholics found a secure home among the South's Protestants. Catholic Bishop John England of Charleston was revered among the city's Protestant population. Unlike in many Northern states, there was little if any violence directed toward Catholics or their institutions. Catholic educational and healthcare institutions were held in high regard by Southerners. During a yellow fever epidemic in Augusta, Georgia the mayor of the city praised the efforts of the nuns and priests of the city in caring for those stricken with the disease and aiming some sharp criticism at certain Protestant clergy who were absent during the epidemic. In defending the reasons for their absence, the Protestant ministers wrote a letter which they requested to be published in the Catholic *Miscellany*, a national weekly published by Bishop John England. Such consideration for Catholic public opinion was unusual in other parts of the United States. Among the many local militia companies of the South were Irish Catholic companies, such as the Jaspers Greens in Savannah. Such a thing was unthinkable in Boston or New York.

One factor that may have accounted for the relatively peaceful accommodation of religious pluralism in the South is what the Southern man of letters, Richard Weaver, termed "the older religiousness of the South." Weaver observed, "For although the South was heavily Protestant, its attitude toward religion was essentially the attitude of orthodoxy." Plural in denominations, evangelical in its dominant mode, but orthodox in belief may have created the conditions friendly toward religious tolerance. This was but one aspect of what Weaver viewed as the South's "medieval heritages." Interestingly, it was not uncommon for some Protestant ministers of the antebellum period to have a copy of Saint Thomas Aquinas's *Summa Theologiae* in their library, or for a Protestant family to have a copy of Thomas a Kempis's, *Imitation of Christ,* or some other Catholic devotional or two on the library shelf.

The South's religious world was turned over by war and Reconstruction. The South's defeat was a devastating test of faith. Northern missionaries, most especially Methodists and Baptists, sensed an opportunity in the wake of the South's defeat. Both the Methodist and Baptist national conferences had split apart over slavery and a myriad of theological matters before the War Between the States. It was deemed an opportune time by some Northern Methodists and Baptists to heal these breaches and influence the future direction of Southern religion. After all, victory in the war seemed to vindicate the Northern Methodist and Baptist view of society, and the federal government was subsidizing the building of churches in the war torn South.

The aims of the Northern clergy, as laid out by George Matton, a Methodist minister from New York, were simple and comprehensive: provide support and succor to those Southerners loyal to the national Methodist Episcopal Church and the federal government, restore social order, instill the habits of cleanliness, industry, economy, purity, and morality on both white and black Southerners. Embedded in these aims were assumptions about both white and black Southerners not atypical among some of the Northern elite. The Presbyterian, Lydia Schofield, was quite adamant that the role of the Northern churches was to change the hearts and minds of Southerners. In part, she hoped to divert Southern preachers from their emphasis upon sin and salvation (read Christian orthodoxy), and to purge from the land the "idol of slavery," which in her view continued to blind Southern ministers. Doing so would bring white Southerners out of their prejudices and uplift the freedman from their "semi-barbaric state."

Southerners had other ideas. On the heels of the war's conclusion, African-Americans left their Baptist and Methodist congregations to set up their own churches with their own ministers. Southern whites were saddened and disappointed by this, but one astute Southern white minister knew what moved African Americans to undertake this secession from the churches, "Disguise it as we may, our colored brethren are disposed to independent action—they want preachers and churches of their own." Northern missionaries initially opposed the establishment of separate African American churches as it undermined their own views on the form Southern religion should

110

take. By 1880, both Northern missionaries and white Southerners found the trend to be beneficial. Northern missionaries were beginning to embrace the widespread support Americans were giving to racial segregation. They also believed that they might exercise greater influence over African Americans if they were away from their former masters. Robert Lewis Dabney, a prominent Southern theologian, argued strenuously against ordaining African Americans in the Presbyterian Church, most especially if such ordinations meant that African American ministers would pastor white congregations. It was an interesting convergence of views among Northerners and Southerners in support of segregated congregations. Northerners, however, did not wield the influence they hoped to with either black or white Southerners. Northern missionaries dismissed Southern resistance, both white and black, to their efforts as evidence of the unregeneracy of Southerners in general. By 1890, Northern missionaries had left the field of Southern missions for more promising endeavors elsewhere.

Fundamentalism, the second wave of Northern religious proselytization, proved far more effective than the first wave. The success of Fundamentalism was due to the shared concerns between Northern and Southern evangelicals regarding the state of Christianity and society during the late nineteenth and early twentieth century. Fundamentalism emerged as a response to the challenges posed by the social gospel movement, theological modernism, liberalism, and the emerging historico-critical exegesis in biblical studies. In the face of these latest trends, which were stripping from Christianity its supernatural claims, Fundamentalists asserted the supernatural character of Christianity, the authority and inerrancy of scripture, the power of holiness to resist temptation, overcome sin, and separate oneself from the world, and the necessity of the Christian to evangelize. Fundamentalists also supported prohibition, traditional gender roles, and were anti-Darwin.

Some innovative ideas were also present in Fundamentalism and became dominant in Fundamentalist circles by the 1940s. This included premillennialism, the belief that Jesus Christ would establish an earthly one thousand year reign after a period of tribulation. Dispensationalism, the belief in God's ordaining of different dispensations in different eras of history. And the rapture, the belief that Jesus would remove his elect from the earth before the great tribulation. These were all recent innovations in the Christian thought and theology and would become an early source of conflict between Fundamentalists and other Christians in the South.

While Fundamentalists offered a powerful critique of modernity, they were also quite adept at using the tools of modern life in spreading their ideas and beliefs. They embraced the concept of "efficiency" they found in the modern ideas of capitalism and American business practice, and some Fundamentalists did view material prosperity as a sign of God's favor. Dwight Moody of Chicago, Lewis Sperry Chafer, a student of Cyrus Scofield whose bible commentary had an enormous influence in Fundamentalist circles, and Amzi Dixon, at that time a rare native Southern Fundamentalist who worked with Dwight Moody, were all skilled communicators and organizers. They began successful bible conferences in the South, made skillful use of the print media, set up enduring schools and seminaries, and were masters of the new media of radio and film. All these men, and others such as Dr. Charles Hammitt of Philadelphia, the mentor of Bob Jones, Sr., played a vital role in the introduction and eventual spread of Fundamentalism in Southern Evangelical circles. The process of evangelizing the South in the new gospel of Fundamentalism was multidimensional. Itinerant preachers came South to lead revivals in the cities and towns of the South. New churches were founded such as Atlanta's Tabernacle Bible Conference (later church), as well as new seminaries and colleges such as Columbia Bible College and Dallas Theological Seminary.

The general reaction of Southern Evangelicals to the Fundamentalist in their midst was ambivalence. On the one hand, Fundamentalists were viewed as allies and brothers in arms in the war against religious liberalization and secularization. Other Southern Evangelicals were not so sure. Some Southerners viewed the Fundamentalists as dangerous theological innovators and suspected that premillennialism, dispensationalism, and the rapture were unorthodox. At one point, Presbyterian congregations refused to hire graduates from Dallas Theological Seminary over these theological issues, and over differences regarding ecclesiology. Southerners were intensely loyal to their denominations and believed that theologically they were in decent shape compared to

Northern Protestant churches. When there were some attempts on the part of Fundamentalists to infiltrate and directly influence the Southern Baptists and Southern Methodists, Southerners were not appreciative and fought to limit Fundamentalist influence in these denominations.

Fundamentalism did win important victories over time in the twentieth century, and as a result changed Southern religion. Mastering the media and endowed with tireless energy in the holding of conferences, revivals, and the production of radio and television programs the Fundamentalists won adherents to their views throughout the South. Calvinism, once muted in the antebellum South in both its religious and secular variants, took on a new and vital form in the twentieth century South. "Once saved, always saved" reintroduced the Calvinist concept of the "elect," as distinct from the sinner. This once uncommon belief in antebellum Southern churches gained much ground in Southern Evangelical circles over the course of the twentieth century. By the 1930s, Southern churches were strangely resistant to Protestant "neo-orthodoxy's" theology of the tragic, as presented by Reinhold Niebuhr and Karl Barth, that emphasized the limits under which man must labor and his utter dependence on God's grace. Contra Ernest Kurtz's flawed but insightful article, "The Tragedy of Southern Religion," Southern Evangelicals of the antebellum period were receptive to the virtue of humility, the recognition of human limitation, and the necessity of grace. The Puritan tendency was at most latent among Southern Evangelicals until the influence of Fundamentalism nudged Southern churches down the road that divides the world into the elect and the sinners. In more recent times the rise of the religious right, the involvement of evangelicals in political campaigns and activism, the unqualified support for the government of Israel, are all striking changes to Southern religion when one takes the long view of things.

Has the wide embrace of the tenets of Fundamentalism brought about the emergence of a Southern Puritan? Yes and No. Without a doubt, there has been weakening, but not a disappearance, of the older religiousness so crucial to Southern religious identity. Not every Southerner, or every Southern Evangelical, black, Hispanic, or white has embraced the tenets and worldview of Fundamentalism. Humility is still a virtue one can find in the South, and those who divide the world into the camps of the godly and the ungodly are not in a majority. Nevertheless, Fundamentalism did successfully reconstruct a substantial portion of Southern evangelicalism. Yet, all forms of Puritanism do secularize as the history of New England and Greater New England illustrates. While the South remains the most religious of the regions of the United States, it is not immune from the rising tide of secularism, neo-paganism, and good old fashioned unbelief. How Southern Fundamentalism interacts with these trends and how it is possibly changed by them will constitute the next great chapter in Southern religion.

THE LATE UNPLEASANTNESS:
MEMORY, MEANING AND UNDERSTANDING

The War Between the States is called by many names, the most genteel being "The Late Unpleasantness." The low country districts of South Carolina, including the environs of Charleston, is the geographic origin of this title for America's most bloody and divisive conflict. There is a deeper significance to the term than a polite and refined attempt to soften an episode of deep human suffering and loss. The phrase contains within it a suggestion that the War and its suffering will pass, and that civilization will survive. In my part of the country, the border South, the term "The War Between the States" is favored, less cultivated, but historically accurate. Others favor the "War of Northern Aggression" or the inaccurate "Civil War" or in other times "The Great Rebellion." The reluctance of Americans outside the scribbling and chattering classes to come to a common agreement on what to call the great conflict of the 1860s is deeply significant. It means that we Americans have no common memory, common meaning, or common understanding of the War. The War remains a point of conflict and division.

Memory, meaning, and understanding are the crucial elements of any people's historical consciousness. These elements are not discrete and separate categories closed off from each other. Rather, they blend one into the other, memory and meaning are the foundations of historical understanding. Memory holds dear the symbols, stories, experiences, and material associations surrounding a historical event. In the concrete sense this includes the flags, monuments, graves, letters, diaries, journals, uniforms, weapons, and oral histories of the War. From these sources of memory people derive meaning, or more dangerously, impose a meaning upon the events associated with the sources of memory. To find meaning means to make sense of what has occurred: Why did the event happen? What were the reasons moving historical actors to pursue certain paths and make particular choices? What are the consequences? Americans are apt to distill the answers to such questions into very compact meanings. Thus, the war meant "a new birth of freedom" or the defense of "states' rights" or "a righteous cause to destroy slavery." The American tendency to produce distilled, simplistic meanings for the momentous events of their history tends to distort our understanding of these events. Our attachment as a people to pragmatism and our relative youth as a country has many advantages, but it leaves us vulnerable to misunderstanding complex phenomena in any number of fields of human endeavor. The War is no exception.

Let us not be too hard on Americans in this regard. The French, an ancient people who are renowned for their detachment when dealing with the complex and the complicated, have yet to come to a collective understanding of the central event in their history, the French Revolution. France is now on republic number five, precariously so, and French historiography remains deeply divided on the meaning and understanding of the French Revolution. Yet, the French Revolution was much more so a conscious act of rupture with the past than even the War Between the States, an historical action that remade the regime even as it consolidated all real political power in the national state. How to best understand such an event is a daunting task.

The Late Unpleasantness has its European "cousins," the unification of Germany, the unification of Italy, and the Carlist wars in Spain, but the presence of American exceptionalism has effectively blocked the construction of an American interpretive framework of the war that incorporates the War Between the States into a larger Atlantic narrative. We view the war not only as an American event, but a singular American event. It is unwise that we do so. It is especially unwise for Southerners to do so.

What is at stake in the battle for the memory and meaning of the War is grave. Power, particularly that power to demonize and marginalize one's opponents, is at stake for the Left. The remaking of American society according to the dictates of Cultural Marxism is also in play. The Left has made considerable progress in achieving these aims. Many people in the South who view themselves as conservatives have come to accept the general outlines of the Left's, and in particular the neo-Abolitionist Left's, meaning of the War. To wit: the War was fought over slavery and only slavery, it signaled a new birth of freedom which found its fullest expression through time in the various "rights" movements of the 1960s to this day. The ending of slavery was only the beginning of the remaking of all American society into a new birth of freedom. The inability of conservatives in general, and many Southerners in particular, to effectively fight the social and cultural transformation of America is due to the fact they agree, at least in part, with this leftist narrative of the War and its meaning. The meaning that the Left has assigned to the War through its Orwellian control of the "approved" memories of that struggle has left Americans with a badly distorted understanding of themselves and their history. For Southerners, it has meant never ending demonization.

The South's bid for independence should be viewed in a larger Atlantic context as one of many important resistance movements against the consolidation of political power in central governments, the resulting social and cultural homogeneity that plagues us, and the rise of the deep state to protect the interests of those political, financial, technocratic, and cultural elites who prattle on about new births of freedom even as they forge new chains for us. Southern memory should admit into its realms the remembrance of those valiant Italians, Germans, and Carlists who opposed the political, economic, and cultural consolidation of their countries. It is a reminder to those of the South that we were not and are not alone in this resistance to tyranny in its many manifestations, and thus the meaning of our resistance is the necessity of assigning limits to political power and resisting when power seeks to violate those limits. Our fight was and is a particularly important part of a larger fight to resist the perpetual revolution that has shaken not only our country, but so many others as well.

About The Author

John Francis Devanny was born in Maryland and received his Ph. D. in history from the University of South Carolina. For over 25 years, he taught a wide range of courses in the fields of history, literature, politics, religion, and economics. He plied his craft at a variety of schools including Catholic schools, an Episcopal school, a non-sectarian school, and the South Carolina Governor's School for the Arts and Humanities. His scholarly essays have appeared in several peer reviewed journals and anthologies. Jeffersonian political and economic thought is his focus, particularly John Randolph of Roanoke, but his work also includes forays into Southern literature and culture. He is currently an adjunct professor of history at Christendom College and an online adjunct instructor in history for Liberty University's graduate program. When he is not teaching or writing, he can be found in the garden; on a good day, he will be in the field or on the stream. He resides in Front Royal, Virginia with his wife Miriam, two of his four adult children, a useless if entertaining cat, and a spoiled Boykin Spaniel named Genevieve.

Available From Shotwell Publishing

If you enjoyed this book, perhaps some of our other titles will pique your interest. The following titles are now available for your reading pleasure... Enjoy!

MARK C. ATKINS
WOMEN IN COMBAT
Feminism Goes to War

JOYCE BENNETT
MARYLAND, MY MARYLAND
The Cultural Cleansing of a Small Southern State

GARRY BOWERS
SLAVERY AND THE CIVIL WAR
What Your History Teacher Didn't Tell You

DIXIE DAYS
Reminiscences Of A Southern Boyhood

JERRY BREWER
DISMANTLING THE REPUBLIC

ANDREW P. CALHOUN, JR.
MY OWN DARLING WIFE
Letters from a Confederate Volunteer

JOHN CHODES
SEGREGATION
Federal Policy or Racism?

WASHINGTON'S KKK
The Union League during Southern Reconstruction

WALTER BRIAN CISCO
WAR CRIMES AGAINST SOUTHERN CIVILIANS

JAMES C. EDWARDS
WHAT REALLY HAPPENED?
Quantrill's Raid on Lawrence, Kansas: Revisiting The Evidence

TED EHMANN
BOOM & BUST IN BONE VALLEY
Florida's Phosphate Mining History 1886-2021 and the Looming Ecological Crisis

DON GORDON
SNOWBALL'S CHANCE
My Kidneys Failed, My Wife Left Me & My Dog Died (I Still Miss That Dog!)

PAUL C. GRAHAM
CONFEDERAPHOBIA
An American Epidemic

WHEN THE YANKEES COME
Former Carolina Slaves Remember Sherman's March FROM the Sea

CHARLES HAYES
THE REAL FIRST THANKSGIVING

T.L. HULSEY
25 TEXAS HEROES

JOSEPH JAY
SACRED CONVICTION
The South's Stand for Biblical Authority

SUZANNE PARFITT JOHNSON
MAXCY GREGG'S SPORTING JOURNALS 1842 - 1858

JAMES RONALD KENNEDY
DIXIE RISING: Rules for Rebels

WHEN REBEL WAS COOL
Growing Up in Dixie, 1950-1965

NULLIFYING FEDERAL AND STATE GUN CONTROL:
A How-To Guide for Gun Owners

JAMES R. & WALTER D. KENNEDY
PUNISHED WITH POVERTY
The Suffering South – Prosperity to Poverty and the Continuing Struggle

THE SOUTH WAS RIGHT!

YANKEE EMPIRE
Aggressive Abroad and Despotic at Home

PHILIP LEIGH
CAUSES OF THE CIVIL WAR

THE DEVIL'S TOWN
Hot Springs During the Gangster Era
U.S. GRANT'S FAILED PRESIDENCY

THE DREADFUL FRAUDS:
Critical Race Theory and Identity Politics

Free Book Offer

Visit **FreeLiesBook.com**

Sign-up for new release notifications and receive a **FREE** downloadable edition of:

Lies My Teacher Told Me:
The True History of the War for
Southern Independence
by Dr. Clyde N. Wilson

and

Confederaphobia:
An American Epidemic
by Paul C. Graham

You can always unsubscribe and keep the book, so you've got nothing to lose!

www.ingramcontent.com/pod-product-compliance
Lightning Source LLC
Chambersburg PA
CBHW060053100426
42742CB00014B/2815